Grover Cleveland:
The Last
Jeffersonian President

Grover Cleveland:
The Last
Jeffersonian President

Ryan S. Walters

Abbeville Institute Press

ISBN: 978-1-7334075-2-6

By the Abbeville Institute Press
P.O. Box 10
McClellanville, SC 29458

To all the Jeffersonian Patriots in both North and South who strive each and every day to restore our Republic of Republics.

Contents

Acknowledgments... I

Preface V

The Jeffersonian Ideal

Introduction XXI

Who Was Grover Cleveland and Why Is He Important?

Chapter 1 1

Grover Cleveland and the South

Chapter 2 19

Grover the Good: Cleveland's Extraordinary Public Character

Chapter 3 43

Businessman's President or Man of the People?

Chapter 4 75

How Cleveland Used Conservatism to End an Economic Panic

Chapter 5 99

How Cleveland's Foreign Policy Upheld Jeffersonian Traditions

Chapter 6 121

Party Destroyer or Defender of Principle?

Afterword... 149

Why History Matters

About The Author 155

Index 157

"The historian is a prophet looking backward."

Friedrich Schlegel

Acknowledgments

A s any author will tell you, a literary work can be successful only with some outside assistance and my book is no exception. Each and every day, young and unproven writers struggle to find publishers for their manuscripts. When this book project first began, I encountered similar obstacles as I embarked on the same lonely trail. After several rejections, I discovered Westbow Press, a division of Thomas Nelson Publishers and I initially published with them.

My original book, *The Last Jeffersonian: Grover Cleveland and the Path to Restoring the Republic*, compared Grover Cleveland and his Jeffersonian policies with modern political problems because I found them to be very similar in many respects. It was simply a way to show the relevancy of history and how historical lessons can be applied to the modern world. It was not a full biography of Grover Cleveland and was never intended to be.

After five years of publication, and more study of the Jeffersonian Ideal, I was graciously invited by Dr. Don Livingston to speak at The Abbeville Institute's Summer School in July 2017 in Charleston, South Carolina. It was there, sitting in the audience as I reflected on my lecture, which was on the Jeffersonian tradition in America, and as I basked in the wisdom of other speakers, like Professor Livingston, Dr. Clyde Wilson, Dr. Brion McClanahan, and many others, I decided to re-issue the book with a new tilt to it, showcasing more fully Cleveland's attachment to Mr. Jefferson and the Jeffersonian Ideal, which was crafted and upheld mainly by Southerners, as well as an additional chapter on Cleveland's attitude and policies directed toward the South, which had been so instrumental in defending and preserving those political traditions.

So, with those thoughts and ideas running through my head, I pitched my proposal to Professor Livingston, and he suggested the up-and-coming Abbeville Press, which was at that very moment looking for scholarly books. And, to my amazement, the project was off and running far quicker than I ever imagined.

I spent some time re-working the manuscript to get it ready for publication, all while I was finishing the final editing for another book, *Remember Mississippi*. If you read the first version of *The Last Jeffersonian*, you will find here some significant changes. I removed all references to contemporary politics, the many comparisons I used to showcase similarities between our world and the late nineteenth century and how Cleveland's policies could be applied to the modern age. I re-wrote the Introduction and the Afterword, added a new Preface chapter, removed the old Prologue and added the bulk of it to the body of the book, trimmed down a lengthy biographical chapter, and added a brand-new chapter entitled "Grover Cleveland and the South." Within the main body chapters, I added new quotes as headers, polished the prose, and added some new information and a few new sub-chapters. Although it grew out of my original book, it is, as you will find, a new book all to itself.

I believe these changes made the book much better. Arranged topically, rather than chronologically, it focuses on the Jeffersonian principles that became the heart and soul of conservatism, and on Cleveland's complete dedication to them. Simply put, Grover Cleveland was the Thomas Jefferson of the late nineteenth century, and he governed like Southerners did throughout the earlier period of Jeffersonian America.

As a historian of American political history, and a recovering academic with many additional years of self-study, which is often more productive, I am by no means an expert. Far from it. When I was writing the original manuscript, and finding myself in the weeds in areas in which I felt inadequate to the task, I sought the aid of experts within a more narrowed field and within disciplines in which I am untrained. Dr. Joseph Salerno, an economist at Pace University in New York City, whom I first met in 2012 at the Ludwig von Mises Institute while delivering a paper at one of their conferences, very kindly examined parts of the manuscript on the cumbersome monetary issues regarding the Panic of 1893. His advice kept me from making several mistakes.

Lawrence W. Reed, the president of the Foundation for Economic Education, and a fellow fan of Grover Cleveland, generously took his time to read the manuscript in its entirety. His advice on numerous points improved the manuscript significantly .

State Senator Chris McDaniel, my good friend and the top conservative in my home state of Mississippi, also read the complete manuscript, even though his legislative and legal workload is enormous. His aid and encouragement helped me through the process, while giving me a much-needed boost of confidence as the book went to press.

Any mistakes within the pages of this book are mine and mine alone.

Ryan S. Walters
Fort Worth, Texas
Spring 2021

Preface

THE JEFFERSONIAN IDEAL

"These principles form the bright constellation which has gone before us and guided our steps through an age of revolution and reformation. The wisdom of our sages and blood of our heroes have been devoted to their attainment. They should be the creed of our political faith, the text of civic instruction, the touchstone by which to try the services of those we trust; and should we wander from them in moments of error or of alarm, let us hasten to retrace our steps and to regain the road which alone leads to peace, liberty, and safety."

—Thomas Jefferson, First Inaugural Address,
March 4, 1801

"The memory of Jefferson's patriotism, conservatism, wisdom, and devotion to everything American should be kept warm in the hearts and minds of his countrymen, and especially of his political followers. The contemplation of these things should serve to check every tendency to follow false and delusive lights, and to tread untried and unsafe paths."

—Grover Cleveland to William E. Burnett,
February 3, 1891

The United States has never been free of political disputes. They have always been with us, even before we had a permanent Constitution, and always will. Yet the struggle that defined our politics began with the ratification of the Constitution, in a sometimes-nasty political fight that resulted in the beginning of our two-party system and the birth of our first two political parties.

In 1787, a young America was very politically divided between two opposing factions – the federalists, or "friends of the Constitution," and the anti-federalists, those who opposed it. After successful ratification, this battle spilled over into an ideological contest between two of President George Washington's cabinet officers and their respective regions: Secretary of the Treasury Alexander Hamilton from New York and Secretary of State Thomas Jefferson from Virginia.

The Federalist Party, or Hamiltonians, believed in a strong central government, a national banking system, fiat currency, a national debt, protective tariffs and internal taxes, direct aid to corporations, loose construction of the Constitution, the suppression of civil liberties, and an internationalist foreign policy.

The Republican Party, or Jeffersonians (not to be confused with the modern-day Party of Lincoln), by contrast, believed in limited government, federalism, sound money, low taxes and tariffs, no national debt, government separation from banks, no subsidies for business, a strict construction of the Constitution, including the protection of civil liberties, and a non-interventionist foreign policy.

Simply put, the Hamiltonians believed in the merits of an energetic national government; Jeffersonians believed in de-centralization and trusted in the people to govern themselves.

Under Washington, Federalist arguments won out over Jeffersonian ones, at least on domestic policy, as Hamilton set out to undo the limited government established by the Constitution, which he called "a frail and worthless fabric." As Hamilton once said to Washington, "we need a government of more energy" and that's what he sought to create by subverting the new Constitution. The new federal government created a national bank (an early forerunner to the Federal Reserve), levied an array of internal taxes, and began running up a national debt, which Hamilton believed would be a "national blessing." By contrast, the Jeffersonian Madison called a public debt a "public curse."[1]

Now consider the great contrast here: Americans had only recently concluded a war of independence against Great Britain, with taxation being a major issue. And considering what Mather Byles had said of a possible break with Britain – "Which is better – to be ruled by one tyrant three thousand miles away or by three thousand tyrants one mile away?" – look at the situation Americans faced under the Federalists: In addition to state and local taxes, citizens now faced taxation from the federal government on several articles, which caused many to wonder just why it was that they had broken from Britain. This was especially true after the Whiskey Rebellion when the national government, under Hamilton's direction, used military force to collect these taxes. What had really changed? Some believed it was worse than it had been under the British. As Murray Rothbard has written, to the "average American, the federal government's assumption of the power to impose excise taxes did not look very different from the levies of the British crown."[2]

By the time of the Adams administration, from 1797-1801, things had gotten even worse. In 1798, the government suppressed civil liberties with the Alien and Sedition Acts, a series of four new laws designed specifically to quash the followers of Jefferson. Three of them dealt with immigration, a crackdown that was solely based on the fact that most new immigrants from Europe were joining the Republicans. Many of the new laws contained sunset provisions that expired soon after the election of 1800, because they would no longer be needed. The fourth, and worst of all, was the Sedition Act, passed just seven years after the ratification of the Bill of Rights, a law that punished political speech, thereby giving the administration the power to punish Jeffersonian newspaper editors. Many were arrested, jailed, and fined, including Benjamin Franklin Bache, grandson and namesake of one of America's most famous Founders.

This all proved too much for the American people, a road they did not wish to travel. So, in the election of 1800, Jefferson and his Republican Party won an overwhelming victory, taking the White House and sweeping both houses of Congress, a triumph Jefferson himself predicted, which stopped Hamilton's big government offensive and killed the Federalist Party, for it never obtained power again. Jefferson called it the "Revolution of 1800," but one of ballots, not bullets.

In his inaugural address, Jefferson laid out his vision for America, one that would consist of "a wise and frugal Government, which shall restrain men from injuring one another, shall leave them otherwise free to regulate their own pursuits of industry and improvement, and shall not take from the mouth of labor the bread it has earned. "This," he said, "is the sum of good government." He then outlined what he considered the "essential principles of our Government":

> Equal and exact justice to all men, of whatever state or persuasion, religious or political; peace, commerce, and honest friendship with all nations, entangling alliances with none; the support of the State governments in all their rights, as the most competent administrations for our domestic concerns and the surest bulwarks against antirepublican tendencies; the preservation of the General Government in its whole constitutional vigor, as the sheet anchor of our peace at home and safety abroad; a jealous care of the right of election by the people—a mild and safe corrective of abuses which are lopped by the sword of revolution where peaceable remedies are unprovided; absolute acquiescence in the decisions of the majority, the vital principle of republics, from which is no appeal but to force, the vital principle and immediate parent of despotism; a well-disciplined militia, our best reliance in peace and for the first moments of war till regulars may relieve them; the supremacy of the civil over the military authority; economy in the public expense, that labor may be lightly burthened; the honest payment of our debts and sacred preservation of the public faith; encouragement of agriculture, and of commerce as its handmaid; the diffusion of information and arraignment of all abuses at the bar of the public reason; freedom of religion; freedom of the press, and freedom of person under the protection of the habeas corpus, and trial by juries impartially selected.[3]

And it was these principles that became the Jeffersonian Ideal, the true principles of the American Revolution.

Jefferson put these principles into practice as the new president. He cut spending, eliminated all internal taxes, repealed the Alien and Sedition Acts while pardoning all those prosecuted under it, and returned fines to the accused out of the treasury. By the time Jefferson left the presidency in 1809, all of Hamilton's taxes had been abolished, to prevent what Jefferson called "the bottomless abyss of public money." The federal budget under the Federalists amounted to some $5 million per year. President Jefferson cut this by more than half, to $2.4 million. The national debt was reduced from $80 million to $57 million. In addition, the treasury accumulated a surplus of $14 million.[4]

Over the next sixty years, with only a few exceptions, the nation was governed by these Jeffersonian principles, operating eventually through what would become the modern Democratic Party. Though it took some time, the Jeffersonians eventually repealed Hamilton's entire program, including the ultimate destruction of the Bank of the United States and the elimination of the national debt under Andrew Jackson. Jeffersonian America was the freest and most prosperous place on Earth. There were no federal taxes on the people, no regulations, no federal police force, and no standing army. Americans had soundly rejected the centralizing ideas of Hamilton and the Federalists, and determined that Jefferson carried the sacred fire of liberty.

But even though Jefferson's principles governed the country for those sixty years, it's easy to sometimes refer to them as "Southern conservatism" or a "Southern philosophy," for it was Southerners who largely crafted them and upheld them. Senator Willie P. Mangum of North Carolina, an Anti-Jackson candidate for President in 1836, wrote that it was Southerners, as the keepers of Jefferson's flame, that were "the real conservators of our political system." The South alone would preserve the Jeffersonian Ideal.[5]

We must not forget, however, that these were, in actuality, American ideals, American principles, and American policies because most Americans believed in them at the time. And even though it was the South that early on dominated national affairs, electing a majority of presidents, House Speakers, and other national leaders, and, by 1860, dominating the Supreme Court, there were many in the North that held strongly to Jeffersonian principles, including presidents and other leaders. The only true nationalist president during the Jeffersonian years was John Quincy Adams of Massachusetts, who did not gain a plurality of popular or electoral votes and whose very election by the House of Representatives was the result of corruption, and who served but one term, like his father before him, because Americans in that day rejected centralization and nationalism.

And, for most Americans both North and South, it was the system of state sovereignty, supported by nullification and secession, that could preserve and peaceably keep the Union together. John C. Calhoun contended "that the great conservative principle of our system is in the people of the States, as parties to the Constitutional compact." Calhoun was using the word "conservative" in its truest sense, meaning to preserve, conserve, and maintain. Senator Mangum believed similarly, writing to a friend and fellow Southerner in 1834 that the "principles that you and I hold to be the only conservative principles of our Federative system, so far from having taken root in the North & the East, are scarcely comprehended by the most intelligent of the National republicans," who were the forerunners to the Whigs and the ideological heirs of Hamilton. "The basis of all party organization in the North & East is naked interest," he continued. "Principles are silly things as contradistinguished from pecuniary interest." New England has a principle, he said, "that we abhor, & believe to be destructive ultimately of our system, in case it shall prevail." And that principle was nationalism.[6]

By the 1850s and 1860s, this view was becoming widespread and the differences between the two sections and the two pervasive philosophies – conservatism and nationalism – more apparent. As Professor Clyde Wilson has written, in his book *The Yankee Problem: An American Dilemma*, the "North had been Yankeeized, for the most part quietly, by control of churches, schools, and other cultural institutions, and by whipping up a frenzy of paranoia about the alleged plot of the South to spread slavery to the North, which was as imaginary as Jefferson's guillotine." As James Henley Thornwell of South Carolina wrote in 1859, "There is at work in this land a Yankee spirit and an American spirit." And that Yankee spirit, decidedly un-American, was working against the Jeffersonian Ideal.[7]

What was this "Yankee spirit"? It came from the old Massachusetts Puritans, a distinct group of people who began increasing in numbers and spreading across the North, so much so that other Northerners, those not of the Puritan line, recognized the influx and resented it. Yankees were the polar opposite of Jeffersonians, which is the philosophy most Americans adhered to during the antebellum period.

The Northern intellectual Orestes Brownson understood the mind of the New England Yankee:

> The New Englander has excellent points, but is restless in body and mind, always scheming, always in motion, never satisfied with what he has, and always seeking to make all the world like himself, or as uneasy as himself. He is smart, seldom great; educated, but seldom learned; active in mind, but rarely a profound thinker; religious, but thoroughly materialistic: his worship is rendered in a temple founded on Mammon, and he expects to be carried to heaven in a softly-cushioned railway car, with his sins carefully checked and deposited in the baggage crate with his other luggage to be duly delivered when he has reached his destination. He is philanthropic, but makes his philanthropy his excuse for meddling with everybody's business as if it were his own, and under pretense of promoting religion and morality, he wars against every generous and natural instinct, and aggravates the very evils he seeks to cure.[8]

This perfectly describes the Hamiltonian, and later Lincolnian, personality, as well as that of the modern-day progressive. And it was this spirit that had captured much of the North by 1860.

Jefferson, as politically astute as he was, saw these differences very early and wrote about them more than six decades before secession, during the darkest days of the Adams administration, in which he served as vice president. In a 1798 letter to his friend John Taylor of Caroline, during the year of the Alien and Sedition Acts, Jefferson complained that the young country was "completely under the saddle of Massachusetts and Connecticut." He added that they "ride us very hard, cruelly insulting our feelings, as well as exhausting our strength and substance." New

Englanders displayed a great "perversity of character," which was a main reason for the "natural division of our parties."[9]

The growing philosophical divide eventually came to a head with the emergence of a purely sectional party, the new Republican Party, conceived in 1854 after passage of the Kansas-Nebraska Act. The party grew rapidly by coalescing many different elements: old Northern Whigs, various abolitionist parties, and anti-Nebraska Democrats.

The South certainly saw the dangers apparent with the Republicans, but some Northerners did as well. "If this sectional party succeeds," wrote Millard Fillmore to James Buchanan in 1856, "it leads inevitably to the destruction of this beautiful fabric reared by our forefathers, cemented by their blood, and bequeathed to us, a priceless inheritance." During his presidency, one also derided by historians, Franklin Pierce realized what Fillmore did about the new party and the divisions it would cause. "The storm of frenzy and faction must inevitably dash itself in vain against the unshaken rock of the Constitution," he said. In other words, if the people stuck to those ideals, embodied in the Constitution, the political storms that lay ahead could be weathered.[10]

By 1860 the Republican Party had taken on a whole new appearance with the addition of vast economic proposals, essentially the old program of Hamilton and Henry Clay's American System. And the nominee for 1860 was not some erratic adventurer but a serious politician who was himself an economic animal – Abraham Lincoln of Illinois, who referred to himself as a "Henry Clay Tariff Whig."

Lincoln was, in fact, a Hamiltonian, who believed in the merits of big government but most particularly in the area of economics. According to Gabor S. Boritt, in his book *Lincoln and the Economics of the American Dream*, if you examine Lincoln's career before the war, well over half of everything he wrote or said was on the subject of economics – protective tariffs, a national bank, fiat currency, and federal funding for internal improvements, most particularly railroad construction. Lincoln always considered himself a Whig – Boritt and biographer David Herbert Donald call him the "Whig in the White House" – and sought to put the plan of his "beau ideal of a statesman," Henry Clay, into policy.[11]

The Republican plan greatly concerned the Jeffersonian South, realizing that the high tariff was designed to enrich the North, deplete the

South, and reward well-connected cronies such as railroad magnates and other corporate hacks, who would also gain federal funding for internal improvements that would also benefit the North, while the National Bank would fund it and be perhaps as crooked and corrupt as it had been under Nicholas Biddle. In short, the new Lincoln government, based exclusively on Hamiltonian principles, would, most assuredly, intervene in the internal affairs of the Southern States and plunder them like never before. As Jerry C. Brewer has written in *Dismantling the Republic*, Northern interests were at work to turn the Jeffersonian republic into a "Consolidated Mercantile Empire."[12]

By November 1860, it was apparent to many Southerners, particularly after the horrors of John Brown's raid the year before, that the country was about to undergo sweeping change with Lincoln and the new sectional party that was concerned only with Northern opinion, principles, ideals, and policies, most specifically economic ones.

In 1861, Southerners, their fears exacerbated by the threats of the North, decided they no longer wanted to be a part of this "new nation" and determined to create a government of their own, one reflecting Jeffersonian principles, and they believed that they had every right to do so, as believers in the right of self-determination of peoples, the very heart of the Declaration of Independence. Their creation of the Confederate States of America sought to save the Jeffersonian Ideal of limited government in America.

The contrast then between the Southern and Northern governments was vast. As the *London Times* opined in November 1861, "The contest is really for empire on the side of the North, and for independence on that of the South, and in this respect we recognize an exact analogy between the North and the Government of George III, and the South and the Thirteen Revolted Provinces. These opinions...are the general opinions of the English nation."[13]

Lincoln, and most presidents after him, being Hamiltonians, established all the central tenants of Hamilton's political thought: a national banking system, a fiat currency, high protective tariffs, an income tax, money for corporations, and the suppression of civil liberties.

The Confederacy, as a government under Jefferson Davis, was founded on Jeffersonian principles, the polar opposite of Lincoln's administration.

The Confederate Constitution was a culmination of Jeffersonian political thought. It was nearly identical to the US Constitution, mainly because Southerners believed it was their heritage, but it did contain numerous important changes, which only made it more Jeffersonian – the rights of the states were greatly strengthened, the powers of the Confederate government were more strictly limited, and the document made it much easier to enact changes and to fight back against federal encroachment.

The War, which lasted four years and, by new estimates, killed a million people, was in actuality a revolution. Lincoln overthrew the Jeffersonian principles that had governed the country in favor of a centralizing role for the federal government. He stretched the Constitution past its bounds, trampled the rights of the Southern states, and made a mockery of the cherished American principle of self-determination. He waged war without congressional consent, illegally blockaded Southern ports, unconstitutionally suspended the writ of habeas corpus, imprisoned tens of thousands of American citizens without charges or trial, seized and censored telegraph offices, shut down hundreds of newspapers while arresting and imprisoning editors, attacked civilians, interfered with the electoral process in several states, and destroyed the voluntary Union of our Founders to replace it with a centralized state.[14]

The governor of Lincoln's home state of Illinois, Richard Yates, wrote of this revolution in 1865. "The war has tended, more than any other event in the history of the country, to militate against the Jeffersonian idea, that 'the best government is that which governs least.' The war has not only, of necessity, given more power to, but has led to a more intimate prevision of the government over every material interest of society."[15]

When Confederate General Richard Taylor, son of former President Zachary Taylor, returned to his Louisiana plantation in 1865, he found that "society has been completely changed by the war. The [French] revolution of '89 did not produce a greater change in the 'Ancien Regime' than has this in our social life."[16]

Historians, even those who lived through the conflict, understood the profound changes the war brought. George Ticknor wrote in 1869 that the war had left a "great gulf between what happened before it in our century and what has happened since, or what is likely to happen thereafter. It does not seem to me as if I were living in the country in which I was born." In short, Lincoln's revolution destroyed the Age of Jefferson.[17]

Modern scholars have also made note of this fact. As Lincoln cult member James M. McPherson points out in *Abraham Lincoln and the Second American Revolution*, "after the war the old decentralized federal republic became a new national polity that taxed the people directly, created an internal revenue bureau to collect these taxes, expanded the jurisdiction of federal courts, established a national currency and a national banking structure. The United States went to war in 1861 to preserve the Union; it emerged from war in 1865 having created a nation. Before 1861 the two words 'United States' were generally used as a plural noun: 'The United States are a republic.' After 1865 the United States became a singular noun. The loose union of states became a nation."[18]

Lincoln and his party, writes historian Heather Cox Richardson, "transformed the United States." Before the war the "national government did little more than deliver the mail, collect tariffs, and oversee foreign affairs. By the time of Appomattox, the United States had changed." Wartime Republicans constructed "a newly active national government designed to promote" a worldview of an industrialized America, with Washington playing an increasingly interventionist role. "A strong central government dominated the post-war nation. It boasted a military of over a million men; it carried a national debt of over $2.5 billion; and it collected an array of new internal taxes, provided a national currency, distributed public lands, chartered corporations, and enforced the freedom of former slaves within state borders." Each of these developments flew in the face of the Jeffersonian Ideal. And as a result, the United States effectively lost its constitutional republic during this War of Northern Aggression and the later period of Reconstruction.[19]

Orestes Brownson wrote of the attitudes prevailing in his section of the country as the war was winding down and reconstruction began. "We have some madmen amongst us who talk of exterminating the Southern leaders, and of New Englandizing the South. We wish to see the free-labor system substituted for the slave-labor system, but beyond that we have no wish to exchange or modify Southern society, and would rather approach Northern society to it, than it to Northern society."[20]

Reconstruction, like the war before it, continued the aim of destroying the old Jeffersonian Union and erecting a new one in its place, one based on federal government control rather than on federalism and individual liberty. Many of the Radical Republicans, the "madmen" referred to by Brownson, like Thaddeus Stevens, sought to ethnically-cleanse the former Confederacy, viewing the South as conquered territory to be treated as such. Senator Zachariah Chandler of Michigan spoke of this inhumane policy directed at Southerners: "A rebel has sacrificed all his rights. He has no right to life, liberty, property, or the pursuit of happiness. Everything you give him, even life itself, is a boon which he has forfeited." Stevens said the South should "be laid waste, and made a desert," then "re-peopled by a band of freemen."[21]

Radical Republicans hated the South and Southern institutions, particularly the Jeffersonian philosophy of government, which they hoped to destroy for good. They wanted the complete subjugation of the region, vindictive punishment of the rebels, the overthrow of all Southern state governments, and the confiscation of all land and homes. Peoples from the North and West would then be sent to the South to repopulate it, ensuring that it would remain firmly Republican and solidly Lincolnian. In other words, they wanted to make the South like the North, just like Brownson had said, sweeping away all vestiges of Southern culture and politics. Such thoughts are certainly revolutionary. Lincoln's Navy Secretary, Gideon Wells, the lone conservative Democrat in the Cabinet, called the Radical plan "an atrocious scheme of plunder and robbery."[22]

And Republicans certainly had the power to get what they wanted. From Lincoln's election in 1860, the GOP held the White House for the next twenty-four years, and the makeup of Congress was nearly as one-sided. From the midterm elections in 1858 until 1888, Democrats managed to control the House for only twelve out of thirty years; the Senate for just four. It seemed as if the "Grand Ole Party" had been and would be in power forever.

But the revolutionary ideas of Radical Republicans did not prevail. Although it seemed as if the war and Reconstruction killed the Jeffersonian Ideal completely, it did receive a brief revival under Grover Cleveland, who saw himself in the mold of the nation's Founders, especially Jefferson, who could reverse the destruction of political institutions the war and Reconstruction had wrought, just as the Sage of Monticello turned back the destructive Federalist tide in 1800.

As president, Cleveland wanted to overturn the Lincolnian revolution and to turn the nation back to the notions of the Founders, what he, like Jefferson, often referred to as "good government." In 1933, the journalist

H. L. Mencken wrote favorably of him as "the last of the Romans."
Congressman Samuel Cox, who would serve as Cleveland's ambassador
to the Ottoman Empire, wrote passionately of a man he admired greatly,
comparing him to a Roman statesman who'd battled Caesar. As he wrote
in his memoirs:

> Rome never needed a Cato more than America needed
> a man of similar qualities, to free her from the gives of
> corrupt politics. This nation has such a man for president.
> While others may falter in duty, he will stand firm and
> true to the principles of the platform on which he was
> elected, and observe and carry out his pledges of reform in
> letter and spirit. His need was so exigent that we may well
> stand appalled at the danger we have escaped, and which
> threatened our free institutions. It needed a statesman as
> courageous as Caesar and as honest as Cato to save our
> liberties from a decadence worse than death.[23]

America had its "Cato" in Grover Cleveland. The future seemed
bright indeed.*

Endnotes

1   Alexander Hamilton to Gouverneur Morris, January 27, 1802, https://founders. archives.gov/documents   Hamilton/01-25-02-0297;   Thomas   DiLorenzo's *Hamilton's Curse: How Jefferson's Archenemy Betrayed the American Revolution and What It Means for America Today* (New York: Crown Forum, 2008); James Madison to Henry Lee, April 13, 1790, https://founders.archives.gov/ documents/Madison/01-13-02-0106.

2   One source for the Mather Byles quote: http://www.newenglandhistorical society.com/mather-byles-bostons-jester-to-the-revolutionary-cause/; Murray N. Rothbard, *Making Economic Sense* (Auburn, AL: Ludwig von Mises Institute, 1995), 162.

3   Jefferson, First Inaugural Address, March 4, 1801.

4   Thomas Jefferson to James Madison, March 6, 1796, in *Writings*, Volume 9, 324.

5   Willie P. Mangum to John Beard, October 7, 1834, in *The Papers of Willie P. Mangum*, Volume II, edited by Henry Thomas Shanks (Raleigh: North Carolina State Archives and History, 1952), 216.

6   John C. Calhoun to Virgil Maxcy, September 1, 1831, in *The Essential Calhoun: Selections from Writings, Speeches, and Letters*, edited by Clyde N. Wilson (New Brunswick, New Jersey: Transaction Publishers, 1992), 299; *Ibid.*, 213.

7   Clyde N. Wilson, *The Yankee Problem: An American Dilemma* (Columbia, SC: Shotwell Publishing, 2016), 9, 1.

8   Orestes Brownson, "Liberalism and Progress," *Brownson's Quarterly Review*, October 1864, in *The Works of Orestes Brownson*, edited by Henry Brownson, Volume XX (Detroit: H. F. Brownson, 1887), 346.

9   Thomas Jefferson to John Taylor of Caroline, June 1, 1798, in Paul L. Ford, ed., *The Works of Thomas Jefferson*, Federal Edition (New York: G. P. Putnam's Sons, 1904), XVIII, 430.

10   Chris DeRose, *The Presidents' War: Six American Presidents and the Civil War That Divided Them* (Guilford, CT: Lyons Press, 2014), 76; Marshall DeRosa, "Franklin Pierce and the War for Southern Independence," in *Northern Opposition to Mr. Lincoln's War*, edited by D. Jonathan White (Waynesboro, VA: The Abbeville Institute Press, 2014), 10.

11   Gabor S. Boritt, *Lincoln and the Economics of the American Dream* (Urbana: University of Illinois Press, 1994); David Herbert Donald, *Lincoln* (New York: Simon & Schuster, 1996).

12 Jerry C. Brewer, *Dismantling the Republic* (Columbia, SC: Shotwell Publishing, 2017), xv.

13 *London Times*, November 7, 1861.

14 For an excellent account of Lincoln's abuses of power, see Thomas J. DiLorenzo, *The Real Lincoln: A New Look at Abraham Lincoln, His Agenda, and an Unnecessary War* (Roseville, CA: Prima Publishing, 2002) and *Lincoln Unmasked: What You're Not Supposed to Know about Dishonest Abe* (New York: Crown Forum, 2006).

15 Governor Richard Yates, Final Message to the Illinois General Assembly, January 2, 1865, *Chicago Tribune*, January 5, 1865, as quoted in Jeffrey Rogers Hummel, *Emancipating Slaves, Enslaving Free Men: A History of the American Civil War* (Chicago: Open Court Publishing Company, 1996), 332.

16 Taylor quoted in James M. McPherson, *Abraham Lincoln and the Second American Revolution* (New York: Oxford University Press, 1991), vii.

17 George Ticknor, as quoted in Morton Keller, *Affairs of State: Public Life in Late Nineteenth Century America* (Cambridge, Massachusetts: Belknap Press, 1977), 2.

18 McPherson, *Lincoln and the Second American Revolution*, viii.

19 Heather Cox Richardson, *The Greatest Nation of the Earth: Republican Economic Policies During the Civil War* (Cambridge, Massachusetts: Harvard University Press, 1997), vii, 1.

20 Orestes Brownson, "Liberalism and Progress," *Brownson's Quarterly Review*, October 1864, in *The Works of Orestes Brownson*, edited by Henry Brownson, Volume XX (Detroit: H. F. Brownson, 1887), 345.

21 John C. Waugh, *Reelecting Lincoln: The Battle for the 1864 Presidency* (Cambridge, MA: Da Capo Press, 1997), 54.

22 *Ibid.*

23 H. L. Mencken, "A Good Man in a Bad Trade," *American Mercury*, Vol. XXVIII, No. 109, January 1933, 127; Samuel S. Cox, *Union-Disunion-Reunion: Three Decades of Federal Legislation, 1855 to 1885.* (Providence, RI: J. A. and R. A. Reid, Publishers, 1885), 683-684. Cox is referring to Cato the Younger (95 BC to 46 BC), who fought the corruption of the Roman Republic under Caesar and whose characteristics are eerily similar to Grover Cleveland—moral integrity, incorruptibility, dedication to duty, distaste for luxury, and a sacred belief in

the past. See Tom Holland, *Rubicon: The Triumph and Tragedy of the Roman Republic* (London: Abacus, 2003), 194–5.

Introduction

WHO WAS GROVER CLEVELAND AND WHY IS HE IMPORTANT?

"True wisdom does not lie in mere practice without principle."

—Thomas Jefferson to John Adams, October 14, 1816

"Your patriotic virtues have won for you the homage of half the nation and the enmity of the other half. This places your character upon a summit as high as Washington's. ... When the votes are all in a public man's favor the verdict is against him. It is sand, and history will wash it away. But the verdict for you is rock, and will stand."

—Mark Twain to Grover Cleveland

WHO WAS GROVER CLEVELAND?

Grover Cleveland's story is a purely American tale of a man of less than modest means, with no political connections, who rose to the highest office in the land. He was born Stephen Grover Cleveland on March 18, 1837, in Caldwell, New Jersey. His family lines stretch back to the earliest settlements in Massachusetts, with the first Cleveland coming to America just fifteen years after Plymouth Rock.

At the age of fourteen, his father moved the family to upstate New York, and it was there that Grover Cleveland would set down his roots.

His father died two years later, and young Grover began to look for future opportunities, working at various jobs, including a two-year stay in New York City, which turned out to be a rather unhappy time. He then determined to head west only to make it as far as Buffalo, the home of an uncle, who persuaded his young nephew to stay with him, a decision that would pay huge dividends in the future.

After Uncle Lewis procured for him a clerkship at a local law firm, and after four years of hard study, Cleveland passed the bar exam and became a practicing attorney in Buffalo. And it was in these early years, during the tumultuous 1850s, that he attached himself to the Democratic Party, even though Uncle Lewis, a former Whig, belonged to the newly formed Republicans. The partners at his firm, all Whigs or Republicans but one, were in a position to exert much influence on the young man.[1]

With a divided firm, it would have been wise for a young up-and-comer to remain neutral, particularly when he could not yet vote. But that was never Grover Cleveland's way. He was one of the most principled of men. He would never remain neutral, not as a law student and not as president of the United States. He openly declared himself a Democrat. In 1856, at the age of nineteen, he worked on the presidential election campaign of Democrat James Buchanan, despite the fact that he was still too young to vote. He marched in torchlight parades and stood outside polling places to hand out ballots. Later in life, he told his close friend Richard Watson Gilder that he chose the Democratic Party because it seemed to him "to represent greater solidity and conservatism." The Republican candidate in 1856, John C. Fremont, "repelled" him, while the Republican campaign struck him "as having a good deal of fuss and feathers about it."[2]

It is interesting to note that Grover Cleveland's first foray into presidential politics was on behalf of James Buchanan, who won the 1856 White House race over Fremont by a close vote. No Democrat would be elected to the office of president of the United States until Grover Cleveland himself some twenty-eight years later.

When the War Between the States broke out, Cleveland was serving as the assistant district attorney for Erie County. Although he was of military age, he did not volunteer to fight for the Union cause as so many Northern men had done. He was quite content to continue his life in Buffalo, far removed from the fighting. As biographer Horace

Samuel Merrill has noted, Cleveland's behavior during the war "was not conducive to political advancement. While others were profoundly moved by the crisis, he remained almost coldly calm."[3]

The situation changed in 1863, as President Abraham Lincoln signed a conscription law instituting a military draft, making the twenty-six-year-old assistant district attorney eligible for the army. And, sure enough, on the first day he was chosen. But he elected not to fight and followed the example of many professionals by hiring a substitute to take his place, which the law allowed. There are a couple of possible reasons for his decision. Perhaps, according to Merrill, "his innate conservatism and inherent independence caused him to resist a popular crusade," which was how the war seemed for many Northerners, especially since Lincoln changed the war's aim that year from one of preserving the Union to liberating slaves. Or, perhaps, he had a much more practical reason. With his older brother William, a minister living in New York City, caring for a family of his own and trying to make a living on a meager pastor's salary, someone had to stay home and care for his mother and sisters. Since Grover had a good job and no obligations of his own, the family decided that he should occupy that role while two other Cleveland brothers joined the fight for the Union.[4]

Authors Larry Schweikart and Michael Allen, though they generally find Cleveland praiseworthy, heavily criticize him for this act, calling him "the first draft-dodger president, no matter the legality of the purchase [of the substitute]." Cleveland's act may have been politically unpopular, but it was well within the law and hardly made him a "draft-dodger," a word that has come to be associated with an act of illegality.[5]

To fulfill his part of the conscription requirements, Cleveland, like so many of his peers, hired a newly arrived Polish immigrant, a seaman named George Benninsky. The conscription act allowed the hiring of substitutes for $300, but Cleveland did not have the money, so he borrowed it from his boss, District Attorney C. C. Torrance. It took him some time to repay the loan, and he was able to do so only after he left his job for private practice. He chose this path even though he had the right, as an assistant district attorney, to procure the services of a convict, who would have readily agreed to fight rather than face the full jail sentence or execution.

The real tragedy of the draft exception was that most substitutes were poor, ignorant immigrants who had little choice in view of the scant options for new arrivals. Arriving in America with no friends, no money, and no job or living arrangements, new immigrants found the army's offer of "three hots and a cot" attractive. Many took the chance, only to end up mangled or dead in a war they had no stake in, as immigrants made up some twenty-five percent of Lincoln's army. But Cleveland's substitute survived the war unharmed, and the two remained acquaintances afterward, with Cleveland helping him financially when he fell on hard times.[6]

As for one of the era's most contentious issues, as a young man Cleveland had a very indifferent attitude toward slavery, precisely because the institution did not directly affect him. He had never come into contact with slavery, and never joined an abolitionist organization. In fact, his family displayed the same indifference. Neither his father nor his mother held abolitionists in high regard, so it's no surprise that Cleveland did not seem interested in the issue.[7]

After losing a race for district attorney in 1865, as most Democrats had become *persona non grata* across the North, Cleveland practiced law until a new political opportunity arose to become Sheriff of Erie County. And even though the county was heavily Republican, he won the election by a slim margin in 1870, taking office on January 1, 1871.

Cleveland's term as sheriff was very successful. The people of Erie County loved the reformer in the sheriff's office and were quite pleased with the results of his three-year tenure. He tackled the rampant corruption and dishonesty associated with his predecessors, working tirelessly to make sure taxpayers weren't being bilked by contractors. He also saved taxpayer funds by personally conducting an unpleasant duty, the hanging of two prisoners sentenced to death, rather than use taxpayer funds to pay an executioner to do it. According to Samuel Horace Merrill, Sheriff Cleveland "conducted the office efficiently and honestly and found the role rather pleasant." Even a political opponent noted that Cleveland had administered the office "with marked efficiency."[8]

After his brief stints in the district attorney's office and as sheriff, Cleveland settled back into what he thought would be a quiet life as a successful attorney, never dreaming that his political career was about to surge with a speed almost unmatched in American political history. Grover Cleveland had a meteoric rise in politics, a climb historian Richard Hofstadter called "rapid and freakish." The remarkable ascent, wrote Henry Jones Ford in 1921, was "without a parallel in the records of American statesmanship."[9]

In the spring of 1881, at the age of forty-four, he was a simple, largely unknown attorney in Buffalo, New York; four years later, in the spring of 1885, at the age of forty-eight, he was inaugurated as the twenty-second president of the United States. The precipitous rise surprised even him. After being in the White House just a few weeks, he spoke to Henry Watterson of the *Louisville Courier-Journal* about the sheer shock of it all. "Sometimes I wake at night and rub my eyes and wonder if it is not all a dream."[10]

In the years between his time as a lawyer and his inauguration as president, his only political experience consisted of a one-year stint as mayor of Buffalo in 1882 and two years of a three-year term as governor of New York, from 1883 to 1885. And in both instances, party leaders and concerned citizens sought his candidacy.

In the fall of 1881, prominent townsmen of Buffalo approached him about the possibility of running for mayor, mainly because of his established reputation as a reformer and a no-nonsense officeholder. He took the opportunity, albeit reluctantly. When he did, he unwittingly set a course for the White House.

As mayor, he set out after the corruption in the city council with such fervor that it attracted the notice of the state Democratic Party. He vetoed numerous wasteful spending measures and took such tough stands against dishonesty in government that he emerged as a serious candidate for governor. He captured the gubernatorial nomination in the summer of 1882 and won election that fall by the largest majority in state history up to that time.

His fierce opposition to corruption and waste continued when he entered the governor's mansion in Albany in January 1883. But just a year and a half into his term at the statehouse, he was approached yet again about seeking higher office. When asked to be a candidate for president of the United States in 1884, he faced many questions about his readiness for such a high office. But once elected, he proved to be an excellent president, though historians continue to place him in the realm of mediocrity.

Cleveland served his first term as president from 1885 to 1889. In his reelection bid in 1888, he faced Benjamin Harrison, a former Union general and grandson of a former president, William Henry Harrison, and lost in the Electoral College, although he won the popular vote.

It was during his first term in the presidency that Cleveland married for the first time, taking as his bride Francis Folsom, the daughter of one of his best friends, the late Oscar Folsom. Mrs. Cleveland, just shy of her 22nd birthday when she wed the president of the United States in the White House, became the youngest First Lady in US history. And it was a young First Lady, after the loss to Harrison, who was responsible for one of the most fascinating stories in American presidential history.

When the Clevelands left the White House soon after the inauguration of Harrison to make way for the new first family, Francis Cleveland made a bold prediction to a member of the staff, a black servant named Jerry Smith. "Now, Jerry, I want you to take good care of all the furniture and ornaments in the house, for I want to find everything just as it is now when we come back again. We are coming back just four years from today." Though the outgoing president probably wouldn't have believed it, nor would he have wanted to entertain such a thought, Francis was determined to be back in Washington.[11]

Many historians, most notably Lewis L. Gould, claim this story is a myth.[12] One source of the tale is from the memoir of Colonel W. H. Crook, the White House Disbursing Officer, who claims to have heard the remark by Mrs. Cleveland, which does not fully substantiate it. But in the correspondence of Richard Watson Gilder, a journalist, poet, and close friend of the Clevelands, there is a letter written by Gilder to Mrs. Cleveland dated November 7, 1888, a few days after the defeat at the polls, in which he attempts to soothe the loss. "Well, perhaps a four years' rest before coming back to the White House for four years more, is better after all! You both need a good, long vacation, and as eight years only is allowed, a four years' vacation is not a bad idea." This letter proves the validity of the story. There can be little doubt that Gilder most likely put that bug in the young ear of Mrs. Cleveland.[13]

Cleveland, though, had no interest in returning to the White House, and was quite content in retirement. But two issues changed his mind: The Republican path of destruction under Harrison and the shift in the Democratic Party away from Jeffersonian principles toward more progressive policies. He determined that he had to run again for a second term to stop the dual threat to the country. In his rematch with Harrison in 1892, Cleveland emerged triumphant, running on pure Jeffersonian policies. He also brought with him a full Democratic Congress, the first time the party controlled both houses of Congress and the presidency since the 1850s. But there were troubles on the horizon as he took office for a second time – an economic depression, labor strikes, and problems in foreign affairs.

WHY IS HE IMPORTANT?

The American public has largely forgotten Grover Cleveland, mainly because he has received scant attention by academic historians and political writers. Only a handful of biographies have been authored, and few academic journals and magazines contain articles with Cleveland as the principal subject.

If something approaching a scholarly consensus has consigned Cleveland to the dustbin, why should we now bother to study him? Since Jefferson was the original Jeffersonian, would he not be a better subject? For one, Cleveland is much closer to modern times and as a result, faced many of the same domestic challenges we do today, including one of the worst economic calamities in our history, a depression similar to those America has faced in modern times. As the nation edged closer to the modern world, Cleveland also faced new problems in foreign policy, but in facing these challenges, he continued to embody Jeffersonian values more fully than anyone in modern times, making him one of the most conservative of presidents and, perhaps, as I hope to demonstrate, the greatest conservative statesman in American history.

As the title of this book proclaims, Cleveland should rightly be regarded as the last Jeffersonian, the last president to espouse the purity of those ideals. Though many may argue the point, what cannot be argued is that he was certainly the last Democrat to serve as president in the Jeffersonian mold and perhaps one of the last national figures in his party advocating the classical liberal persuasion, now a relic of a forgotten past.

I am not the only writer who has advocated this thesis. David N. Mayer, a scholar of Thomas Jefferson, also regards Cleveland as the "last Jeffersonian," as do historians Clyde Wilson and Brion McClanahan in their book *Forgotten Conservatives in American History*. Economics Professor Thomas J. DiLorenzo labeled him "the last good Democrat," while Paul Whitefield, in *Investor's Business Daily*, dubbed him "the last libertarian president." Conservative historians Larry Schweikart and Michael Allen point out in *A Patriot's History of the United States* that he was "the last small-government candidate the Democrats would ever run" for the presidency. Cleveland's most recent biographer, Jeffrey K. Smith, termed him the "last conservative Democratic president." And although many might contend that Warren Harding, Calvin Coolidge, and Ronald Reagan had many Jeffersonian qualities, Cleveland should be considered, without question, the last authentic Jeffersonian president. He is deserving of serious study by historians, conservative scholars, and the general public.[14]

I became seriously interested in Grover Cleveland in my first semester of graduate school at the University of Southern Mississippi in the fall of 2001. Being assigned the task of finding a suitable topic for my master's thesis, I initially chose Cleveland and drew up a research prospectus that focused on his tariff policy. However, I eventually settled on a theme more in line with my field of study at the time, the politics of Antebellum Mississippi. But Cleveland never strayed far from my mind, and I eventually decided to write my doctoral dissertation on his political life, as I broadened my scope to include the political history of nineteenth-century America. I purchased biographies and collections of Cleveland's speeches, writings, and letters for study in my very limited free time.

In the course of my research, I found myself captivated by Cleveland's political courage, character, honesty, and strict adherence to political principles, all extreme rarities today. These characteristics are particularly admirable when you consider that the post–Civil War era was one of widespread dishonesty and selfishness. And yet there was absolutely no hint of corruption in Grover Cleveland. As mayor of Buffalo, he fought and defeated the corrupt ring that controlled the city. As governor, he stared down Tammany Hall, the great New York Democratic political machine and a major engine of corruption. During his first run for the presidency in 1884, his political opponents, unable to tag him as corrupt in an age of unbridled deceitfulness, instead questioned his morality. But in so doing, Republicans succeeded only in demonstrating that he was a man of great morals, integrity, and goodness. Some in the press even labeled him "Grover the Good."

Cleveland was perhaps the most honest man ever to occupy the White House and certainly the most straightforward in the century following his departure from office in 1897. Even his political enemies conceded his honesty. This was a major reason Democrats turned to him in 1884. Yet he was not a man of extraordinary talent or ability. Biographer Allan Nevins stated it best, writing that "in Grover Cleveland, the greatness lies in typical rather than unusual qualities. He had no endowments that thousands of men do not have. He possessed honesty, courage, firmness, independence, and common sense. But he possessed them to a degree other men do not."[15]

And because he possessed moral character to such a degree, he would never involve himself, or his campaigns, in the "politics of personal destruction" that is so prevalent in our day. In fact, he would not tolerate his campaign managers engaging in such practices during his 1884 presidential race with the inherently corrupt James G. Blaine. When a scandal broke that might embarrass and humiliate Blaine's wife, Cleveland ordered his managers to accept Blaine's side of the story and drop the matter, an unthinkable act in the history of American political campaigning.

Cleveland was also one of the most philosophically consistent statesmen in American history. He remained the same, no matter what office he held or sought. Unlike today's politicians, whose morals and platforms change with the wind, Cleveland stuck to his principles. He held so fast to the Jeffersonian Ideal that he often likened it to religion, oftentimes referring to it as "my Democratic faith."

And he kept his campaign promises to reform government. Cleveland was a man and statesman who said what he meant and meant what he said, willing to lose an election rather than betray his cherished ideals, which he did in his presidential reelection bid in 1888. Such traits make him, perhaps, the greatest statesman in American history.

Like Jefferson, he was a fierce advocate of economy and accountability in government. In Buffalo, he was known as the "Veto Mayor"; in Albany, the "Veto Governor"; and in Washington he continued as the "Veto President." In the previous 100 years of presidential history, from George

Washington to Chester A. Arthur, Cleveland's immediate predecessor, twenty-one prior chief executives cast a total of 204 vetoes. But, in his first term alone, Cleveland vetoed 414 bills, mainly extravagant spending measures. His second term saw the rejection of another 170 bills, including forty-nine on his last day in office, giving him a total of 584 in eight years, the most by far of any president until FDR, who eclipsed him by bypassing Washington's unofficial two-term tradition. And of Cleveland's many vetoes, Congress overrode only seven. Unlike our more recent presidents, Cleveland aggressively used the veto pen to keep the federal government within its constitutional and fiscal bounds.

In matters pertaining to the Constitution and constitutional interpretation, Cleveland strongly advocated strict construction, following the original meaning of the Founders, not the progressive "living document" theory that was becoming more prevalent in his day. In his many veto messages to Congress, Cleveland echoed a consistent theme: "I can find no warrant for such an appropriation in the Constitution." To him, like Jefferson, the president had just as much right and authority to interpret the Constitution as did the Supreme Court, and he exercised that power rigorously.[16]

At the start of his second term, Cleveland faced a severe economic depression, known as the Panic of 1893. Though economic statistics of that time were not as plentiful as they are today, the limited data suggests, and many economists and historians agree, that the downturn was one of the worst of the nineteenth century and even rivaled the Great Depression in its severity, especially in the area of unemployment. President Cleveland responded to the emergency in an entirely different manner than one would expect from modern presidents. Unlike a majority of his presidential successors who did everything they could when economic problems arose, Cleveland did not mobilize the full powers of the federal government to fight the depression. There was no talk of handouts for the millions out of work, estimated to be as high as 18 percent nationwide, nor was there any discussion of bailouts for the 16,000 businesses that went bankrupt during the depression's first year, the 500 banks that closed, or the seventy railroads that went into receivership.

The government under Cleveland stopped the inflation that caused the downturn, cut taxes and spending, and allowed the free market to correct itself. As a result, the crisis was short-lived and did not devolve into a "Great Depression" that lasted more than a decade. However, this has not stopped many historians from raking him over the coals for his seemingly uncaring attitude toward those hit hardest by the panic, yet his actions were honorable, just, and in perfect keeping with Jeffersonian principles.

Because of his excellent statesmanship, Cleveland should be of particular importance for Americans today. He provides us with an outstanding example not only for our presidents but for state and local officials as well. He was a superb officeholder and managed the affairs of his local and state offices, that of sheriff of Erie County, mayor of Buffalo, and governor of New York, with as much careful attention as he gave his White House duties. He was also well-liked by the public, winning record-breaking majorities in his victories as mayor and governor as well as a plurality of the popular vote in three successive presidential elections, a feat equaled only by Andrew Jackson and Franklin D. Roosevelt, and all because he stuck to his principles.

But today Cleveland has been shunned, if not outright forgotten. It doesn't help that he served in an era that academic historians have characterized as one of weak and mediocre presidents, those chiefly falling between Abraham Lincoln and Theodore Roosevelt, a time when Congress held most of the influence. Cleveland, though, was far from a weak or mediocre president. Richard Hofstadter has written that Cleveland "stood out, if only for honesty and independence, as the sole reasonable facsimile of a major president between Lincoln and Theodore Roosevelt."[17]

Most of the chief executives during this period can be regarded, in the words of an old political science professor of mine, "postage-stamp presidents," for if they had not appeared on postage stamps no one would know who they were. Rutherford B. Hayes, James A. Garfield, Chester A. Arthur, and Benjamin Harrison are generally not on the lips of most Americans when thinking of their presidential favorites. Cleveland, by contrast, far outclassed all presidents in the late nineteenth century and should, by any reasonable account, rank among the top five most effective presidents. He was determined to keep the country on a proper heading, the course set forth by the Founders, no matter what direction Congress or the courts sought to steer it.

Professional historians, however, most often place President Cleveland in the realm of mediocrity. In articles discussing presidential greatness, he is usually never mentioned. In many presidential polls, he generally ranks in the top twenty but typically never in the top ten, the threshold for greatness and near-greatness. Of all the major historical surveys, he ranked in the top ten just once, coming in at number eight (the "near-great" category) in Arthur M. Schlesinger Sr.'s 1948 poll in *Life* magazine, the first such study ever undertaken. Schlesinger repeated his poll in 1962, this time in the *New York Times*, but Cleveland had slipped to eleventh place, generally an "above average" rating.[18]

In a 1981 poll conducted by historian David L. Porter, Cleveland finished fifteenth, an "average" ranking. In 1982, the *Chicago Tribune Magazine* posted the results of a poll in which Cleveland finished thirteenth. Scholars Robert K. Murray and Tim H. Blessing conducted their own presidential performance study, published in 1982 in the *Journal of American History*. Cleveland came in at number seventeen, again in the "above average" category. Murray and Blessing note that Cleveland has fallen consistently in polls from 1948, where he stood at number eight, to their poll, which listed him in seventeenth place. "Cleveland is rated more harshly by the younger historians than by the older historians," they write, and "will probably not rise above his current ranking as older historians die off." This is particularly true since the older generation of historians tended to be more conservative than their younger counterparts. A more recent survey conducted in 2005 by the more conservative *Wall Street Journal* in conjunction with the Federalist Society pegged Cleveland at number twelve, his latest listing in the "above average" category.[19]

But in the end, Murray and Blessing's analysis has been proven correct, as more recent polls have not been nearly as sympathetic. In a 2002 Siena College Research Institute survey, Cleveland ranked twentieth, just as he did in a C-SPAN President's Day survey in 2009. The poll of sixty-two historians for C-SPAN also ranked each president in ten separate categories, where Cleveland also remained largely in the middle. He ranked highest in "Public Persuasion," coming in at number seventeen, and lowest in "Relations with Congress," at twenty-seventh. In the important categories of "Crisis Leadership" and "Economic Management," he ranked twentieth and twenty-first respectively.[20]

On July 1, 2010, Siena College Research Institute released its latest presidential survey. Cleveland again, as he did in 2002, ranked at number twenty, five spots *behind* Barack Obama, who had served just eighteen months in office when the poll was taken. This review by 238 scholars also ranked each president in twenty separate categories, everything from background and experience to communications and handling of the economy. Cleveland ranked nineteenth in overall leadership and highest in the categories "Avoided Crucial Mistakes," at number fourteen, in "Relations with Congress" at fifteen, and "Party Leadership" at sixteen. In his handling of the economy he ranked twenty-second, close to the twenty-first spot he polled in the C-SPAN survey. But even though many historians praise him for his legendary honesty, strangely he placed nineteenth in "Integrity," meaning there were eighteen presidents that scholars believe were more sincere than Grover Cleveland.[21]

Although these findings are perplexing, two of the most puzzling categories in both the C-SPAN poll and the Siena College survey were those dealing with leadership and economic management. Cleveland's lower rankings are most peculiar since he managed the Panic of 1893 with considerable skill and under intense pressure while maintaining law and order, which had begun to break down, and placing the nation on the road to economic recovery far better than did FDR, who ranked second and fifth in those respective categories in the C-SPAN poll, and first and third in the 2010 Siena College survey. It is puzzling that a president who managed to keep the United States mired in a severe depression for more than a decade as much of the world was coming out of it, while using the opportunity to transform a capitalistic nation into a social welfare state, received such high rankings. Perhaps this says more about the scholars being polled than it does about their rankings.

Other, more recent scholarly examinations by intellectuals in non-historical fields have generally provided a more favorable ranking. Ivan Eland, the director of the Center for Peace & Liberty at the Independent Institute, in his book *Re-carving Rushmore: Ranking the Presidents on Peace, Prosperity, and Liberty* (2009), graded the presidents according to how their policies promoted peace, ensured prosperity, and safeguarded liberty. Eland ranked Cleveland at number two, his highest placement ever. But such praise is limited in academic circles.[22]

So, for a myriad of reasons, Grover Cleveland ranks low in presidential greatness, at least in the eyes of most academic historians and political scholars. Perhaps there is a simple reason for this disrespect, aside from purely ideological ones. Historians Schweikart and Allen, who hold a more favorable opinion of Cleveland, referring to him as a "presidential giant," write that "Republicans have ignored him because he was a Democrat; Democrats have downplayed his administration because he governed like a modern Republican," meaning he was far too conservative, and Jeffersonian for their tastes. Even Woodrow Wilson, as a historian, made note of this fact. "You may think Cleveland's administration was Democratic. It was not. Cleveland was a conservative Republican."[23]

This book, however, is meant to show Grover Cleveland as the great Jeffersonian statesman he was, and is not a full biography of the man. It examines how Cleveland, as a public official, dealt with the major issues of his day during his capacity as a public servant. The issues tackled within these pages are as relevant today as they were in his time – public character and behavior of our candidates; the role of government in the everyday lives of the people; the burden of taxation; the distribution of wealth; government involvement in an economic depression; monetary policy; and complex foreign affairs. As a nation and a people, we shouldn't continue to ignore our political forebears, especially great statesmen such as Grover Cleveland; we should embrace him. He is the embodiment, indeed the last one, of the Jeffersonian Ideal, a tradition that Jefferson himself saw as a "bright constellation" that would guide our future path. May we continue to follow their sage advice.

Endnotes

1   Denis Tilden Lynch, *Grover Cleveland: A Man Four-Square* (New York: H. Liveright, Inc, 1932), 37; Charles H. Armitage, *Grover Cleveland As Buffalo Knew Him* (Buffalo: Buffalo Evening News, 1926), 4.

2   Lynch, 38; Richard Watson Gilder, *Grover Cleveland: A Record of Friendship* (New York: The Century Co., 1910), 224.

3   Horace Samuel Merrill, *Bourbon Leader: Grover Cleveland and the Democratic Party* (Boston, 1957), 11.

4   *Ibid.*; H. Paul Jeffers, *An Honest President: The Life and Presidencies of Grover Cleveland* (New York: Harper Collins, 2000), 30.

5   Larry Schweikart and Michael Allen, *A Patriot's History of the United States: From Columbus's Great Discovery to the War on Terror* (New York: Sentinel, 2004), 448.

6   Alyn Brodsky, *Grover Cleveland: A Study in Character* (New York: St. Martin's Press, 2000), 28; George F. Parker, *Recollections of Grover Cleveland* (New York: The Century Co., 19011), 32.

7   Merrill, 11–12.

8   Merrill, 12; Armitage, 55; Jeffers, 34.

9   Richard Hofstadter, *Age of Reform* (New York: Vintage, 1960), 233; Henry Jones Ford, *The Cleveland Era: A Chronicle of the New Order in Politics* (New Haven: Yale University Press, 1921), 42.

10 Henry Watterson, *"Marse Henry": An Autobiography.* 2 volumes (New York, 1919), II, 118.

11 Allan Nevins, *Grover Cleveland: A Study in Courage* (New York: Dodd, Mead & Company, 1932), 448. Nevins's book, the best of the Cleveland biographies, won the 1933 Pulitzer Prize; W. H. Crook, *Memories of the White House: The Home Life of Our Presidents From Lincoln to Roosevelt* (Boston: Little, Brown and Company, 1911), 198.

12 See Lewis L. Gould, "Grover Cleveland," in Alan Brinkley and Davis Dyer, eds., *The American Presidency: The Authoritative Reference*, 244.

13 Crook, 198; Richard Watson Gilder to Francis Folsom Cleveland, November 7, 1888, *Letters of Richard Watson Gilder*, edited by Rosamond Gilder (Boston: Houghton Mifflin Company, 1916), 165.

14 David N. Mayer, The Mayer Blog, "Rating the US Presidents," http://users.law.capital.edu/dmayer/index.asp; Thomas DiLorenzo, "The Last Good Democrat," Lewrockwell.com, July 8, 2004; Paul Whitfield, "Grover Cleveland, The Last Libertarian President," *Investor's Business Daily*, August 31, 2011, http://news.investors.com/Article/583350/201108311413/Grover-Cleveland-The-Last-Libertarian-President.htm; Schweikart and Allen, *A Patriot's History*, 455.

15 Nevins, *Cleveland*, 4.

16 Cleveland, Veto of Texas Seed Bill, February 16, 1887, James D. Richardson, *A Compilation of the Messages and Papers of the Presidents*, 13 volumes. (New York: Bureau of National Literature, 1897), XI, 5142-5143.

17 Richard Hofstadter, *The American Political Tradition* (New York: Vintage, 1948), 232.

18 *Life*, November 1, 1948; *The New York Times*, July 29, 1962.

19 *Chicago Tribune* magazine, January 10, 1982; Robert K. Murray and Tim H. Blessing, "The Presidential Performance Study: A Progress Report," *Journal of American History* (December 1983), 540, 541, 543, 545; *Wall Street Journal*, September 12, 2005. The *Wall Street Journal*/Federalist Society study has been published in book format, *Presidential Leadership: Rating the Best and the Worst in the White House*, edited by James Taranto and Leonard Leo (New York: Free Press, 2004).

20 Siena College Research Institute, Siena College, Press Release, August 19, 2002; C-SPAN, Historians Presidential Leadership Survey, February 16, 2009, www.cspan.org.

21 Siena College Research Institute, Siena College, Press Release, July 1, 2010.

22 Ivan Eland, *Re-carving Rushmore: Ranking the Presidents on Peace, Prosperity, and Liberty* (Oakland, CA: The Independent Institute, 2009). In Eland's list, John Tyler ranked number one.

23 Schweikart and Allen, *Patriot's History*, 446; Wilson quoted in Vincent P. De Santis, "Grover Cleveland," in Morton Borden, ed., *America's Eleven Greatest Presidents* (Chicago: Rand McNally, 1971), 164.

Chapter 1

GROVER CLEVELAND AND THE SOUTH

"Equal and exact justice to all men, of whatever state or persuasion, religious or political."

—Thomas Jefferson, First Inaugural Address, March 4, 1801.

"I have faith in the honor and sincerity of the respectable white people of the South. ... I am a sincere friend of the negro."

— Grover Cleveland, Address to Southern Educational Association, New York City, April 14, 1903

On March 4, 1885, the long-ruling Republicans watched a Democrat take the oath of office for the first time since 1857. Since James Buchanan gave way to Abraham Lincoln four years later, a quarter century of GOP rule, resulting in corruption, profligate spending, high taxes, and ever-expanding government, had become the norm. Republicans had used the absence of the Jeffersonian South to re-make the country as they desired, implementing programs and policies that Southerners had always rejected.

Lincoln and his party, in the Revolution of 1861, militarily conquered the South in four years and controlled most of the region until 1877 when the final Union troops were removed, thus allowing them to opportunity to rule as they chose. After 1877, Northern leaders shamed the rest of the country into keeping Republicans in power. And in all that time the South lagged far behind, both economically and politically. Before the war, the South possessed the richest states in the Union, while Southerners dominated the national government; after the defeat of the Confederacy, the South did not produce a single national leader for the remainder of the century and fell to last place in wealth. The political shunning stemmed mainly from the North's great anger over the war and the continued use of their oft-used "bloody shirt" tactics to win elections.

But on a spring day in 1885 the sun shone brightly on the South, as a Jeffersonian Democrat became the nation's 22nd president. And Southerners were overjoyed about having a Jeffersonian in the White House. The inauguration was festive, as Southerners came in large numbers, bands played "Dixie," and a former Confederate general rode in the inaugural parade. One reporter from the Atlanta *Constitution* noted a "feeling here to-night stronger than I ever saw it before, that the war is over." This was not necessarily a reference to the actual violent war that concluded twenty years before but the quarter century political war, as one Democratic official declared, "The election of Grover Cleveland to the Presidency of the United States marks the dawn of a new era in our national history." It would be an era when the South was, once again, back in the Union as an equal partner.[1]

A friend of Jefferson Davis wrote to the former Confederate president upon reading Cleveland's inaugural address in the newspaper, joyous that the new chief executive "will be the nearest approximation of 'Old Hickory' since the Civil War." Indeed, Cleveland, like Andrew Jackson, was seen as a fearless president for the common man. "Cleveland is a man of the people," wrote the Atlanta *Constitution*. "He combines more fully than any other man the elements of reform, and ... the people feel they can safely look to him for the ability to plan reforms in public affairs and the courage to carry them out."[2]

Down in New Orleans, the *Daily Picayune* editorialized that "Mr. Cleveland is a popular favorite. He is the people's candidate. No man, in manner and utterance, is farther from being a demagogue. He seems to be talking to the people and for the people. No man in the country today is more beloved by the masses of the people, and the secret of it is that they believe he is their friend."[3]

The South also saw in Cleveland a president who could heal the sectional divide, a decades-long rift that had yet to mend due to the seemingly never-quenching anger in the North. Henry Watterson, the editor of the Louisville *Courier-Journal*, penned an article for the *North American Review* just three months before Cleveland's first inauguration entitled "The Reunited Union." Watterson's hope was for sectional reconciliation. "The election of Mr. Cleveland to the Presidency," he wrote, "sweeps away all sectional distinctions and lines. It brings the South back into the Union and the administration. It gives [the South] the opportunity, which it ought to embrace, of impressing itself upon the national policy. It invests it with actual power and the responsibility that belongs to power, and bids it show its real character as a political entity and force."[4]

The South certainly had that hope. The *Telegraph and Messenger* of Macon, Georgia was sincerely hopeful that the election of Grover Cleveland "had killed sectionalism," although a number of Southerners did not buy it simply because they did not believe the more radical element in the North would ever allow it. But many had faith, like the North Carolina Tar Heel Josephus Daniels, who would later serve in the Woodrow Wilson administration as Secretary of the Navy. He praised Cleveland as "the Democratic Moses who would lead his party into the Promised Land." His election as president "gladdened and heartened the people of the South. They felt they were back in the Union their fathers had helped to found and could again sit down at the government table as equals." Cleveland would end "the exclusion of Southern men from a voice in the government of their country."[5]

This same biblical theme was on the mind of a young Missouri politician named Champ Clark, a future House Speaker and presidential candidate, who first came to Congress during Cleveland's presidency. Clark also thought of Cleveland as "the Moses of Democracy who had led them through the Red Sea and the Wilderness into sight of the Promised Land, but also the Joshua who had brought them safely into Canaan, flowing with milk and honey."[6]

Another young journalist, North Carolina's Walter H. Page, who would later serve as ambassador to Britain under Woodrow Wilson, described Cleveland as "an honest, plain, strong man, a man of wonderfully broad information and of most uncommon industry. He has always been a Democrat. He is a distinguished lawyer and a scholar on all public questions. He is as frank and patriotic and sincere as any man that ever won the high place he holds. He is as unselfish as he is great."[7]

When Cleveland named Hoke Smith of Atlanta to the Cabinet during his second term, an attorney from Los Angeles wrote his congratulations: "I am proud that we have an incoming administration of the affairs of the Government that will give the South an opportunity to show the Nation that the Southern boys are able to take their stand among the great Statesmen of our country." With such a man as Grover Cleveland "at the head of affairs, and with such advisers as he is placing around him, I am sure that our party, and our cause can not fail."[8]

And Grover Cleveland was as good as his word. Just as Watterson had written, Cleveland did desire sectional reconciliation to bring the South back into the Union as an equal, to end the strife and division that had been ongoing for decades, and to roll back everything the Republicans had done for the previous twenty-five years. To the South he wanted to assure "good government to the people and complete reconciliation between all sections of the land."[9]

In the first act of bringing the South more fully into the government, President Cleveland named two dyed-in-the-wool Southerners to the Cabinet and, for the most important cabinet post, that of Secretary of State, he named a strong Southern sympathizer. The South had virtually no representation in the executive branch since before the war, with the only post-war exception being David M. Key of Tennessee, named Postmaster General by Rutherford B. Hayes, an appointment made only as part of the Compromise of 1877 that handed Hayes the White House in the disputed election with Samuel J. Tilden.

Cleveland's two Southern nominees, though, were not just typical politicians who just happened to reside south of the Mason-Dixon Line; he chose two prominent ex-Confederates, and high-ranking ones at that. For attorney general, the new president named Augustus H. Garland of Arkansas, who did not serve in the Confederate army but in both houses of the Confederate Congress. After the war, Garland had to fight for his right to resume the practice of law, since the US Congress, in an act passed in 1865, banned former Confederates from the bar. The case, *Ex parte Garland*, made it to the US Supreme Court, which, after hearing Garland's arguments, struck down the act as an unconstitutional Ex Post Facto law. Denied the right to serve in the US Senate in 1867, Garland was elected to the governorship in 1874, and after Reconstruction was able to take a seat in the US Senate in 1877.[10]

Cleveland's other choice would lead the Interior Department, Lucius Quintus Cincinnatus Lamar of Mississippi, a long-serving statesman later featured in John F. Kennedy's Pulitzer Prize-winning book, *Profiles in Courage*. Lamar had high hopes for Cleveland and stumped for him during the 1884 campaign. "I think that the interests of the South are with the country at large in voting for Cleveland," he said in one speech.[11]

Before the war, Lamar had been a professor of mathematics at the University of Mississippi, then a member of the US House until the election of Lincoln. He then resigned from Congress to serve as a delegate in the Mississippi Secession Convention. And while serving in that capacity, Lamar wrote the secession ordinance that withdrew Mississippi from the Union. During the war he served in the Confederate army as a colonel and was later sent on several diplomatic missions for President Davis on behalf of the Confederate government. After the war, he served in the US House once again, then a term in the US Senate before receiving the call from President Cleveland.[12]

But Lamar would see promotion once again during Cleveland's first term. In the summer of 1887, upon the death of Justice William B. Woods, Cleveland created another political firestorm when he named Lamar to the vacancy on the US Supreme Court. Naming such a prominent former Confederate to the cabinet was one thing; naming him to a lifetime seat on the High Court would be a different matter, for the North would almost certainly oppose his confirmation with a vengeance. Yet in Cleveland's mind this was another important step in bringing the South more fully into the Union.

Senator George F. Hoar, a fierce Northern Republican from Massachusetts who would vote against him, personally liked Lamar, calling him "one of the most delightful of men," who was "far-sighted" and possessed "infinite wit and a great sense of humor." Lamar, though, was the quintessential Southerner of his day, a man who believed it "was a great misfortune for the world that the Southern cause had been lost." Yet, despite that opinion, Hoar admired him. "He stood by his people," he wrote of Lamar in his memoirs, "in their defeat and in their calamity without flinching or reservation." And Hoar believed that Lamar "desired most sincerely the reconciliation of the sections, that the age-long strife should come to an end and be forgotten, and that the whole South should share the prosperity and wealth" of the country.[13]

The opposition to Lamar did not arise simply because he was from the South, at least that's what many Northerners claimed, or because they did not believe he was a decent man. For Senator Hoar, his opposition was "not because I doubted his eminent integrity and ability, but because I thought that he had little professional experience and no judicial experience." Other Senators, like Shelby M. Cullom of Illinois, expressed a similar sentiment. Yet this excuse for opposition seems untruthful, as five of the Court's sitting justices at the time also had no prior judicial experience.[14]

Republican newspapers also attacked Lamar's nomination with a vengeance, but not so much with the "bloody shirt," the age-old Northern campaign device of reminding voters of the late war and those they said had started it. Instead, like Northern Senators, they used other tactics. The *Chicago Tribune* assailed Lamar's views on labor, while the *San Francisco Chronicle* believed Lamar leaned "naturally and spontaneously to the side of the strong against the weak. He is a friend of monopolies." Much of the GOP opposition stemmed from the belief that Lamar would interpret the Constitution, not with a nationalistic viewpoint to which Republicans were accustomed, but with one leaning toward the old strict, states' rights construction.[15]

Despite the political protests, Cleveland knew Lamar's quality. During the confirmation fight, he told Henry W. Grady of the Atlanta *Constitution* that Lamar "cannot decide a thing wrong. His temperament is such that when he considers a question he is obliged to decide it right. I have never seen this quality so marked in any other man." And the president lobbied hard for his confirmation. After months of Senate foot-dragging, he asked Senator Cullom of Illinois to help speed the process along so he could find a replacement for Interior: "I wish you would take up Lamar's nomination and dispose of it. I am between hay and grass with reference to the Interior Department. Nothing is being done there;

I ought to have some one on duty, and I can not do anything until you dispose of Lamar."[16]

Cleveland did get some help from the other side of the isle. Senator William M. Stewart of Nevada, a Silver Republican, thought Northern rejection of Southerners amounted to discrimination and did not believe Lamar's status as a former Confederate should disqualify him. "The Judiciary Committee found him otherwise qualified," he wrote, "but reported that his participation in the rebellion ought to prevent his confirmation." Should the Senate reject him for this reason, it would set "a direct precedent for the rejection for any Federal office of every man in the South who had participated in the rebellion," which was most likely what the North had in mind. Stewart favored Lamar's confirmation and was pleased when the Senate finally gave its consent, saving it "from the disgrace of granting amnesty and then withdrawing it; and of pledging equality of civil and political rights and afterward violating that pledge."[17]

Despite the fierce Northern opposition, including Cullom and Hoar, the Senate confirmed Lamar by the narrow margin of 32 to 28 on January 16, 1888, making him the only Mississippian to sit on the United States Supreme Court. Writing years later, Senator Hoar admitted that he had "made a mistake" in opposing the Mississippian and former Confederate. Though he did not serve on the High Court for long, just five years, Justice Lamar "wrote a few opinions which showed his great intellectual capacity for dealing with the most complicated legal questions," Hoar wrote. Lamar left his post only with his death on January 23, 1893.[18]

For Secretary of State, Cleveland named Senator Thomas F. Bayard, Sr., a member of the famed Bayard family from Delaware. And Bayard's family was truly remarkable:

His great-grandfather, Richard Bassett, signed the Constitution. His grandfather, James A. Bayard, the elder, served in both the House of Representatives and the Senate and cast the deciding vote for Thomas Jefferson in the 1800 election. His uncle, Richard H. Bayard, served in the Senate and as charge d'affaires to Belgium. His father, James A. Bayard, the younger, served in the Senate and resigned his seat in 1864 due to his manly opposition to the Lincoln administration but later accepted another appointment in time to cast a negative vote in the Andrew Johnson impeachment trial.

Though not a Southerner, Bayard assumed his father's seat in the US Senate in 1869 and was very sympathetic to Southerners, opposing what he called the "Radical Party" in the North and its "wretched catalogue of wrongs" inflicted upon the South, and held true to Jeffersonian principles of government. The South could only be too happy about Cleveland's choice of Bayard. As Brion McClanahan has written, while in the Senate, the "Southern delegation respected Bayard for good reason. He was one of them, a man who understood the Republican regime to be the antithesis of American political principles."[19]

In his second term, Cleveland named two more Southerners of the Old Confederacy to his Cabinet. William L. Wilson of Virginia, who had previously served twelve years in the US House from a West Virginia district and who authored the controversial Wilson-Gorman Tariff Act of 1894, was named Postmaster General. Wilson was one of Cleveland's favorites and the president spent a great deal of time with him at the White House discussing a litany of issues.[20]

The other was Hilary A. Herbert, an eight-term Alabama congressman who would head the Navy Department. Herbert greatly admired Cleveland for the courage and "unflinching tenacity with which he held to his beliefs." He also praised Cleveland for helping to end sectionalism by bringing North and South more closely together. Many historians contend that the event that did the most to heal sectional bitterness was the Spanish-American War in 1898 because, for the first time since the Mexican War in the 1840s, Northerners and Southerners fought together on the same side. But for Herbert it was, in actuality, Cleveland's invocation of the Monroe Doctrine in 1895 in a dispute with Britain over Venezuela. President Cleveland's message, wrote Herbert, "struck a cord in the hearts of Congressmen from the North and the South that caused them to stand together for their country as one man."[21]

While in his first term in the White House, Cleveland decided to make a symbolic gesture of goodwill toward the South. Acting on a recommendation from the Secretary of War, the president decided to return captured Confederate battle flags to their respective Southern states. The move, though, provoked anger from the nation's leading Union veterans group, the Grand Army of the Republic (G.A.R.), which boasted a membership of 400,000 former troops. And with his promotion of former Confederates to high office, many Northerners were fearful that the South, through Cleveland, was attempting to re-establish Southern political dominance, the status it enjoyed before the war.

When the news broke of the flag order, Cleveland faced an avalanche of hateful invective from across the North. The *New York Tribune* called the flags "mementos of as foul a crime as any in human history." Senator Joseph Hawley suggested they be burned instead, for they were nothing more than flags taken from "our misguided brothers and wicked conspirators." Governor Joseph B. Foraker of Ohio used the issue in his reelection campaign, stating in a telegram: "No rebel flags will be surrendered while I am governor."[22]

The commander of G.A.R., Lucius Fairchild, who lost an arm at Gettysburg, spoke harshly of the president: "May God palsy the hand that wrote the order! May God palsy the brain that conceived it, and may God palsy the tongue that dictated it!" General Sherman privately hinted at his displeasure with the commander-in-chief. Writing to his brother, Senator John Sherman, he pointed out that "Mr. Cleveland is President, so recognized by Congress, Supreme Court, and the world" so he could not criticize him openly. But neither Cleveland nor Secretary of War Endicott could return the flags since they "never captured a flag" and "did not think of the blood and torture of battle."[23]

As the controversy persisted, things were becoming more heated by the day. The Grand Army's national encampment that year was to be in St. Louis, Missouri, and the group had already invited the president to visit the camp and speak to the veterans. The city's mayor also sent Cleveland an invitation. But after the flag flare up, the president received threats of violence from members of G.A.R., so he declined both the invitations. To the mayor he wrote that he was "hurt by the unworthy and wanton attacks upon me growing out of this matter, and the reckless manner in which my actions and motives have been misrepresented both publicly and privately," as well as by the "threats of personal violence and harm" coming from "scores of misguided, unbalanced men." Yet if the angered veterans at the national encampment wanted to "denounce me and my official acts," he wrote, "I believe they should be permitted to do so, unrestrained by my presence as a guest of their organization, or as a guest of the hospitable city in which their meeting is held."[24]

The political heat arising from the flag issue became so great that President Cleveland was forced to quietly rescind the return order before the flags could be shipped south. The North, unlike the South, had still not gotten over the war. In 1905, President Theodore Roosevelt returned the flags without fanfare and with a unanimous vote by Congress, including many of those who had so vigorously opposed Cleveland's order, demonstrating the opposition was more about politics than anything else.[25]

As for the Grand Army of the Republic, which was as responsible as any group in the country for fomenting sectional hostility and hatred, Cleveland did not hold a high opinion of the organization, at least what he believed were the worst elements of it. The good that is in the organization, the president wrote in a private letter, "is often prostituted to the worst purposes." It has been "played upon by demagogues for partisan purposes, and has yielded to insidious blandishments to such an extent that it is regarded by many good citizens ... as an organization which has wandered a long way from its original design." The group's objectives, he believed, were "partisan, unjust, and selfish."[26]

In the early fall of 1887, President Cleveland embarked on a trip that would take him through the Midwest and parts of the South, including the original Confederate capital of Montgomery, and provide him the opportunity to speak before huge crowds that came from afar to see him and perhaps shake his hand. In Memphis, more than 100,000 Southerners traveled from several of the surrounding states to greet Cleveland. In Nashville, he visited the widow of President James K. Polk; in Atlanta, he dined with former Confederate general John B. Gordon. There was even talk of a movement to bring Jefferson Davis to Georgia to attend an event with Cleveland, but no such meeting ever took place, although the president, in a private letter, hinted that a meeting would not have been refused.[27]

But in a move that might be seen as a revelation of his true feelings, when Melville Fuller, whom Cleveland would appoint Chief Justice of the US Supreme Court in 1888, insisted the president visit Lincoln's tomb as he passed through Illinois, Cleveland refused to do so. Whether his decision reflected his own thoughts, or was simply political pandering to his base in the South, tactics which Cleveland had never been known to exhibit, we will never know, but throughout his tour of the South, President Cleveland never showed any feeling but genuine affection for Southerners as members of the American family.[28]

Cleveland's magnanimous attitude was also on display the year before when he traveled to Virginia and addressed citizens at the state fair in the former Confederate capital of Richmond. In his remarks, he praised the state and its rich, proud history, its traditions, its "true greatness," and the "toil and ingenuity of her people." The state, he told the crowd, was "the Mother of Presidents, seven of whose sons have filled that high office," and on that day greeted "a President who for the first time meets Virginians upon Virginia soil." He pledged to the people of Virginia, and of the entire South, that his administration "is pledged to return" for their hard work and ingenuity "not only promises, but actual tenders of fairness and justice, with equal protection and a full participation in national achievements." The past, he said, is where the relationship between North and South had been "estranged and … interrupted," but "your enthusiastic welcome" of the president "demonstrates that there is an end to such estrangement, and that the time of suspicion and fear is succeeded by an era of faith and confidence."[29]

And his affection for the South and Southerners did not exclude honoring the former Confederacy and its military heroes. In the spring of 1887, Confederate veterans in the Association of the Army of Tennessee invited Cleveland to the battlefield at Shiloh to attend the unveiling of a statue of General Albert Sidney Johnston, killed there twenty-five years before. The president's official duties prevented him from making the trip but he did send a gracious letter praising Johnston for his "conspicuous valor," "military ability," and for exhibiting the "highest personal character." Every citizen of the country should take pride in the character of General Johnston, the president believed. Southerners had not heard such gracious words from a president in a generation.[30]

Yet it must be noted that Cleveland's affection for Southerners included both races. Racial issues were always a hot-button topic, even in Cleveland's day, and the South was the region most affected since the vast majority of blacks in America lived below the Mason-Dixon Line. As a nineteenth-century white man, and given the prevailing attitudes of the day, Grover Cleveland did not interfere with the "Jim Crow" system of segregation prevalent in the South, nor did any other president for that matter. But the system was also dominant in the North. In fact, in his epic book *The Strange Career of Jim Crow*, C. Vann Woodward points out that the system of segregation, though generally blamed on the South, "was born in the North and reached an advanced age before moving South in force." Northerners "made sure in numerous ways that the Negro understood his 'place' and that he was severely confined to it." Both political parties in the North, Democrats and Republicans alike, "vied with each other in their devotion" to white supremacy. "It is clear," concludes Woodward, "that when its victory was complete and the time came, the North was not in the best possible position to instruct the South, either by precedent and example, or by force of conviction, on the implementation of what eventually became one of the professed war aims of the Union cause – racial equality."[31]

According to scholar John Chodes, systematic segregation came not as a result of Southern racism but government policy, and at a time when Northerners exclusively ran Washington. Segregation "is the result of federal policy from 1865 to 1900 to divide the white and black races and to promote discord and hatred for political advantage." They accomplished this during Reconstruction via the Union League, the Freedman's Bureau, the Bureau of Education, and various congressional acts.[32]

In his only brush with segregation as a policy, Cleveland, as governor of New York, signed a bill that would "retain the colored schools separate and distinct from the whites" in New York City. The bill's intent was to block the New York City public schools from consolidating the black and white schools, and Governor Cleveland approved it when it was "strongly urged before me that separate schools were of much more benefit to the colored people than mixed schools." In fact, the superintendent of the black schools in the city wanted to keep the segregated arrangement. So Cleveland was only perpetuating a system that had a long history in his section of the country decades before he became governor and president.[33]

But in other areas involving race, Cleveland was a little ahead of his time and has been considered by most a racial moderate. He did not hold obsessive racist thoughts and did as much he could for the plight of black Americans. While some historians have condemned Cleveland as being a typical racist president who gave no place to blacks either in the White House or in his administration, those notions are plain wrong. He named a black man, Winston Sinclair, as White House steward, a position that made him responsible for supervising the property and the grounds around the executive mansion, which was an important job. As president, wrote Clarence Lusane, author of *The Black History of the White House*, Cleveland "represented a transitional moment in the relationship between African Americans and the White House, and African Americans and the nation." Nearly all of Cleveland's biographers, even some of his most sympathetic, overlook these facts.[34]

In 1887, Cleveland replaced Frederick Douglass, a Republican serving as Recorder of Deeds for Washington, D.C., the highest-ranking African American in the country, with another black man, James Monroe Trotter of Mississippi, who had escaped slavery to Ohio via the Underground Railroad. Douglass, who had met with the president on several occasions, wrote fondly of Cleveland in his memoirs. "I have no cause of complaint against him" for the removal, wrote Douglass, while "there is much for which I have reason to commend him. I found him a robust, manly man, one having the courage to act upon his convictions, and to bear with equanimity the reproaches of those who differed from him. He never failed while I held the office under him, to invite myself and wife to his grand receptions, and we never failed to attend them." And Cleveland was not "less cordial and courteous than that extended to the other ladies and gentlemen present," he wrote, and "he was too noble to refuse me the recognition and hospitalities that my official position gave me the right to claim."[35]

Cleveland also greatly admired Booker T. Washington, black leader and founder of the Tuskegee Institute in Alabama, who also had great admiration and respect for the president. Washington had given a tremendous speech at the Atlanta Cotton Exposition in the fall of 1895 and he sent a copy to Cleveland, which greatly impressed the president. "Your words cannot fail to delight and encourage all who wish well for your race," he wrote to Washington in a letter of thanks. Because of "your utterances," American blacks should "gather new hope and form new determinations to gain every valuable advantage offered them by their citizenship."[36]

"From that time until the present," wrote Washington in his memoirs, *Up From Slavery*, "Mr. Cleveland has taken the deepest interest in Tuskegee and has been among my warmest and most helpful friends." The president has "shown his friendship for me in many personal ways, but has always consented to do anything I have asked of him for our school." Cleveland gave personal donations and used his "influence in securing the donations of others." Washington did not believe Cleveland "is conscious of possessing any colour prejudice. He is too great for that."[37]

When Cleveland, along with his Cabinet, visited the Cotton Exposition, he met personally with Washington, who "became impressed with his simplicity, greatness, and rugged honesty." Having the opportunity to meet Cleveland on future occasions, Washington wrote that "the more I see of him the more I admire him." Along with Washington, Cleveland "spent an hour in the Negro Building, for the purpose of inspecting the Negro exhibit and of giving the coloured people in attendance as opportunity to shake hands with him." The president "seemed to give himself up wholly, for that hour, to the coloured people. He seemed to be as careful to shake hands with some old coloured 'auntie' clad partially in rags, and to take as much pleasure in doing so, as if he were greeting some millionaire." He also signed an autograph for everyone who sought it.[38]

For Grover Cleveland, as it was for Booker T. Washington, the goal was to bring blacks, many of them less than a generation removed from slavery, into the fullness of American society. Just as with Native Americans, Cleveland believed the government should work to assimilate blacks completely into civilization. And the best way to do that for black people, he felt, was through educational opportunities. In fact, Cleveland referred to black education as "the proper solution of the race question in the South." The efforts of Booker T. Washington and the Tuskegee Institute "point the way to a safe and beneficent solution." If blacks "in their mature years" are to "exercise ... the right of citizenship," he wrote in a private letter, "they should be fitted to perform their duties intelligently and thoroughly." To this effort, Cleveland contributed not just rhetoric but financial contributions as well.[39]

Throughout his time in public office, Grover Cleveland took Jeffersonian principles to heart, most particularly the notion of "equal and exact justice to all men," regardless of who they were. The days of slavery were long gone; the days of warfare between the states were likewise over. It was time for North and South to reconcile and move forward as one nation, and he saw himself as one who could begin the process of reconciliation and reunion, despite the pressures from those who would not let go of a disagreeable past.

Endnotes

1   R. Hal Williams, "'Dry Bones and Dead Language': The Democratic Party," in H. Wayne Morgan, ed., *The Gilded Age* (Syracuse, 1970), 129.

2   E. G. W. Butler to Jefferson Davis, March 7, 1885, in *Jefferson Davis, Constitutionalist: His Letters, Papers, and Speeches*, edited by Dunbar Rowland (Jackson, MS: Mississippi Department of Archives and History, 1923), IX, 350; *Atlanta Constitution*, July 12, 1884.

3   New Orleans *Daily Picayune*, June 23, 1892 and July 20, 1892.

4   Henry Watterson, "The Reunited Union," *North American Review* (January 1885), 22-30.

5   Macon *Telegraph and Messenger* quoted in a letter from Chas. Herbst to Jefferson Davis, April 3, 1885, in Rowland, *Davis, Constitutionalist*, Volume 9, 360-362; Josephus Daniels, *Tar Heel Editor* (Chapel Hill: University of North Carolina Press, 1939), 200.

6   Champ Clark, *My Quarter Century of American Politics*, 2 volumes (New York: Harper & Brothers, 1920), II, 231.

7   Burton J. Hendrick, *The Life and Letters of Walter H. Page*, 2 volumes (New York: Doubleday, 1923), I, 40.

8   J. H. Johnson to Hoke Smith, February 16, 1893, in Hoke Smith Papers, University of Georgia.

9   Cleveland to the People of Charleston, South Carolina, June 18, 1886, in Allan Nevins, ed., *Letters of Grover Cleveland, 1850-1908* (Boston: Houghton Mifflin Company, 1933), 113-114.

10   Leonard Schlup, "Augustus Hill Garland: Gilded Age Democrat," *Arkansas Historical Quarterly* (Winter, 1981), 338-346.

11   Edward Mayes, *Lucius Q. C. Lamar: His Life, Times, and Speeches, 1825-1893* (Nashville, TN, 1896), 454.

12   *Ibid.*

13   George F. Hoar, *Autobiography of Seventy Years.* 2 volumes (New York: Charles Scribner's Sons, 1903), II, 177.

14 Hoar, 177; Shelby M. Cullom, *Fifty Years of Public Service: The Personal Recollections of Shelby M. Cullom* (Chicago: A. C. McClurg & Co, 1911), 227.

15 Willie D. Halsell, "The Appointment of L. Q. C. Lamar to the Supreme Court," *Mississippi Valley Historical Review* (Dec. 1941), 403-404.

16 Henry W. Grady to Lamar, October 29, 1887, Mayes, 521; Cullom, 277.

17 William M. Stewart, *Reminiscences of William M. Stewart of Nevada*, Edited by George Rothwell Brown (New York, 1908), 308-309.

18 Cullom, 277; Hoar, 177.

19 Brion McClanahan, "Thomas F. Bayard, Sr.," Abbeville Institute Review, https://www.abbevilleinstitute.org/blog/thomas-f-bayard-sr/.

20 Festus P. Summers, ed., *The Cabinet Diary of William L. Wilson, 1896-1897* (Chapel Hill, 1957), vii.

21 Hilary A. Herbert, "Grover Cleveland and His Cabinet At Work," *Century Magazine*, March 1913, 740-744.

22 John M. Taylor, "Grover Cleveland and the Rebel Banners," *Civil War Times Illustrated*, September 1994.

23 Jack Beatty, *Age of Betrayal: The Triumph of Money in America, 1865-1900* (New York: Vintage Books, 2008), xiii; William T. Sherman to John Sherman, June 26, 1887, The *Sherman Letters: Correspondence Between General and Senator Sherman from 1837 to 1891*, edited by Rachel Sherman Thorndike (London, 1894), 375.

24 Cleveland to the Mayor of St. Louis, MO, July 4, 1887, in George F. Parker, ed., *The Writings and Speeches of Grover Cleveland* (New York: Cassell Publishing Company, 1892), 398-401.

25 John M. Taylor, "Grover Cleveland and the Rebel Banners," *Civil War Times Illustrated*, September 1994.

26 Cleveland to E. W. Fosnot, October 24, 1887, Nevins, *Letters*, 160.

27 Nevins, *Cleveland*, 319-320; Brodsky, 197-198.

28 Cleveland to Wilson S. Bissell, September 2, 1887, Nevins, *Letters*, 149-151.

29 Cleveland, Speech at the Virginia State Fair, October 12, 1886, Parker, *Writings and Speeches*, 159-160.

30   Cleveland to Walter H. Rogers, April 1, 1887, Nevins, *Letters*, 132-133.

31   C. Vann Woodward, *The Strange Career of Jim Crow* (Oxford, 1955), 17-18, 20.

32   John Chodes, *Segregation: Federal Policy or Racism?* (Columbia, SC: Shotwell Publishing, 2017), 6.

33   Cleveland to G. A. Sullivan, August 27, 1887, Nevins, *Letters*, 149.

34   Kenneth T. Walsh, *Family of Freedom: Presidents and African Americans in the White House* (Boulder, Co, 2011), 8; Clarence Lusane, *The Black History of the White House* (San Francisco, 2011), 241.

35   Frederick Douglass, *Life and Times of Frederick Douglass*, in *The Frederick Douglass Papers*, edited by John R. McKivigan, Series Two, Volume 3, Book 1 (New Haven, Yale University Press, 2012), 391-392.

36   Raymond W. Smock, *Booker T. Washington: Black Leadership in the Age of Jim Crow* (Chicago, 2009), 161; Cleveland to Booker T. Washington, October 6, 1895, in Booker T. Washington, *Up From Slavery* (New York, 1907), 227.

37   Booker T. Washington, *The Story of My Life and Work* (New York, 1901), 156; Cleveland to Washington, *Up From Slavery*, 228.

38   Washington, *Up From Slavery*, 227-228.

39   Cleveland to Isaiah T. Montgomery, January 14, 1891, Parker, *Writings and Speeches*, 344-345; Cleveland, Speech to the Southern Educational Association, April 14, 1903, Bergh, 423-425.

Chapter 2

GROVER THE GOOD: CLEVELAND'S EXTRAORDINARY PUBLIC CHARACTER

"Is it the less dishonest to do what is wrong, because not expressly prohibited by written law? Let us hope our moral principles are not yet in that stage of degeneracy."

—Thomas Jefferson to John Wayles Eppes,
September 11, 1813

"In many respects ... Mr. Cleveland made the country a good president. He was of absolute integrity, honest and faithful in the discharge of his official duties, and would not tolerate graft, fraud, or corruption in public places or among government officials."

—O. O. Stealey, Louisville *Courier-Journal*

The comportment of a candidate in a political campaign is a good indicator of how a person will behave once in office. As Senator John C. Calhoun once said, "We may rest assured that those who will play false to get power will play false to retain it." History is a testament to this irrefutable wisdom.[1]

CAMPAIGN CONDUCT

Political campaigns in the nineteenth century were nasty and bitter. By 1884, Cleveland's first run at the presidency, Republicans had possessed the White House for twenty-four successive years and had no intention of ever giving it up to an opposition party they considered synonymous with rebellion. The War Between the States had all but destroyed the Democratic Party, painted as it was with the brush of treason. Like Germany after World War One, Democrats received all the blame for the bloody conflict. If any Democrat, North or South, tried to gain political power in any branch of the federal government, Republicans quickly brandished their "bloody shirt" campaign tacatic in retaliation, reminding voters who was at fault for the hundreds of thousands of battlefield deaths and the sundering of the Union.

When seeking a candidate for president in 1884, Democrats, after six consecutive presidential defeats, decided to try someone new, a younger reform candidate not tied to the Washington crowd. Even though they had failed with two New York governors in the past, Horatio Seymour in 1868 and Samuel J. Tilden in 1876, they reached out to the sitting governor of New York in 1884, Grover Cleveland, specifically because of his personal character and conduct in office. With nearly two decades since the end of the war, and the public souring on public corruption, Cleveland seemed a perfect fit for the mood of the country.

During his service as mayor in Buffalo and governor of New York, he led crusades against public corruption, and his honest, straight-talk campaigns impressed members of both parties, as well as independents. In every race he ran, Cleveland gained votes from the opposing party, winning record-breaking majorities in his mayoral and gubernatorial contests. Just as the 1980s saw the emergence of Reagan Democrats, the 1880s beheld Cleveland Republicans. And since the "bloody shirt" card finally seemed to be losing steam by the mid-1880s, Cleveland's reform credentials and his vote-getting ability made him an attractive candidate who might be the one to finally take down the Grand Old Party.

The campaign, as usual, would prove a nasty affair. Republicans depicted their Democratic counterpart as the "town drunk," a "debaucher," a "lecherous beast," a "hangman," an "obese nincompoop," and a "drunken sot." But Grover Cleveland would not play their dirty game. He had character, such that even those who loathed him had to acknowledge it. His great character came from his strong Christian upbringing, being raised in a spiritual home with a father and older brother who were both pastors in the Presbyterian Church and a mother who was equally grounded in the faith. Cleveland believed in the power of prayer, feeling "so much safer" with his mother's invocations, which he believed "had so much to do with my success." Even his career in the great game of politics did not cause him to abandon his personal conduct.[2]

When placed at the head of the Democratic presidential ticket in 1884, he had every reason to toss ethics to the wind and conduct a mudslinging campaign in order to win. This became more imperative since he would face the quintessential establishment candidate in James G. Blaine of Maine, the GOP nominee. Blaine had been in politics his entire adult life it seemed, and, what's more, he was good at it. As a young man he served in the Maine state legislature, including a stint as speaker, and then in the US House, where he again sat in the Speaker's chair. He also served as a US Senator and finally as Secretary of State under James Garfield. He was, without question, the most popular Republican in the country. When his name was announced at the Republican National Convention that summer, pandemonium ensued from the multitude of self-professed "Blainiacs."

But with such distinguished service came the inevitable scandals. In short, Blaine was notoriously corrupt, a man who, in the words of reformer Carl Schurz, "wallowed in the spoils like a rhinoceros in an African pool." In his worst scandal, while serving as House Speaker, Blaine got involved in a crooked Arkansas land deal. In exchange for company stock, Blaine ensured that a rail line received a land grant from the government. The situation only grew worse when Blaine's past letters surfaced discussing the illicit arrangement in detail. At the end of each post, he instructed the recipient to "burn this letter." But his correspondent did not, and the letters became public, though Blaine was never convicted of any crimes or censured for his conduct. In politics, however, the scam stuck to him like glue, denying him the presidential nomination in both 1876 and 1880. He finally won out in 1884 only because it was "his turn," an affliction that seems to be instilled in both political parties.[3]

With Blaine's potential troubles, and a public fed up with corruption, Cleveland could coast into the White House, provided the Democrats ran a smooth campaign free of mud thrown in their direction. But scandal soon struck Cleveland in a personal way. Opponents alleged that while residing in Buffalo as a young man he had fathered a child out of wedlock more than a decade before. Such news terrified his campaign managers, who tried to coax him to lie to save his chance at the presidency. But Cleveland refused, sending an instructive telegram to Charles Goodyear, one of his supporters. "Whatever you do, tell the truth," he told him.[4]

To this day it has never been conclusively proven whether Cleveland fathered the child. The woman in question, Maria Halpin, named the baby Oscar Folsom Cleveland, supposedly after his father. But complicating the matter was the fact that Oscar Folsom, a law partner and good friend of Cleveland's, might also have had a dalliance with Miss Halpin. So, to whom did the boy belong? One likely explanation may be found in another certain fact: Folsom was married, and Cleveland was not. It is quite possible that Cleveland simply took the blame for the child rather than see one of his closest friends fall from grace with a shameful divorce. Cleveland paid child support for the first year of the boy's life, and finally, with the help of a local judge, placed him in an orphanage because Halpin had become an alcoholic. Folsom, though, had died in a carriage accident in 1875, a year after the child's birth, and could not come to his friend's defense. Cleveland himself had always remained silent on the matter.[5]

Charles McCune, a reporter for the *Buffalo Courier*, a Democrat-friendly newspaper, wrote a story alleging that Cleveland had, in fact, been protecting the good name of his dear friend Folsom. Given this opportunity, Cleveland could have done what many politicians would have never hesitated to do: throw his deceased friend under the bus to protect his chance for the presidency. Folsom had been dead nearly a decade, so hurting him personally would not be a factor. But, in a related twist, Cleveland was also the ward for Folsom's daughter, Francis, who he would marry in 1886. So, perhaps, he had an even more personal reason for not wanting to trash Folsom's name.

After seeing the newspaper story, Cleveland angrily wrote a friend about the allegation. "Now is [McCune] crazy, or does he want to ruin anybody? Is he fool enough to suppose for a moment that if such was the truth (which it is not, so far as the motive for silence is concerned) that I would permit my dead friend's memory to suffer for my sake?" Much to the chagrin of his campaign managers, he would not tarnish the reputation of his friend to win the White House. He would continue to take responsibility for the child, election be damned. In the end, though, it did not hurt Cleveland's reputation with the American public.[6]

Having one's reputation smeared by a political opponent, especially as embarrassing as Cleveland's mishap, generally begets retaliation. Cleveland's campaign managers found some serious personal dirt on Blaine they sought to use to tarnish the Republican nominee, perhaps as payback for the Halpin scandal. But if the information were leaked to the press, it would have been deeply embarrassing for Blaine's wife, Harriet. In short, the allegation was that the Blaines had not been legally married when their firstborn son arrived, an appalling disgrace in those days. Cleveland aides brought a man into the governor's office who claimed to have documentation of the alleged infidelity. Cleveland paid him for the evidence and then dismissed him. He then asked his assistants if all facts of the scandal were now in his personal possession. When they affirmed that he had all in existence, Cleveland shredded the documents and threw the pieces into the fireplace where the roaring blaze would forever destroy it. "The other side can have a monopoly of all the dirt in this campaign," he said, and ordered the matter dropped. There would never be an "October Surprise" in any campaign Cleveland was involved with.[7]

Another very common, if not expected, tactic in the nineteenth century was for campaign managers to make promises to state leaders in order to gain their support for the presidential nomination and in the general election. Party leaders who made significant contributions to a victorious presidential campaign held it their sacred right to suggest nominees for cabinet officers and other high-ranking officials or even claim a top spot for themselves. The notion that campaign managers made deals to win support had pervaded American presidential politics from the beginning, since it was unfashionable for candidates to actively campaign for the White House. With the candidates absent from both the convention and the campaign trail, managers generally took it upon themselves to make promises, keeping the candidate in the dark. Once elected to the presidency, the White House's new occupant then discovered that the top spots in their new administration had largely been filled.

Candidates often told their managers to never engage in such tactics but they always did. Abraham Lincoln instructed his managers to "make no contracts [that] bind me," but then found that promises had been made in order to gain enough support for him in 1860. Later, after discovering the deals, Lincoln angrily said his managers had "gambled me all around, bought and sold me a hundred times." After his retirement, President Benjamin Harrison told Teddy Roosevelt that when he won the presidency in 1888, he "found out that the party managers had taken it all to themselves. I could not even name my own cabinet. They had sold out every place to pay election expenses."[8]

In rare instances, some nominees made the secret deals themselves to assure support. James Garfield, who belonged to the "Half-Breed" faction of the Republican Party, desperately needed the support of Stalwart leader Roscoe Conkling in New York to overcome opposition from the Tammany Hall machine in New York City. Garfield promised Conkling control of the state's patronage at a meeting with Conkling's surrogates at a Fifth Avenue hotel in August 1880, just before the kickoff of the fall campaign. Most often, however, such assurances were generally made on the candidate's behalf at closed-door meetings in smoke-filled backrooms away from the prying ears of newspaper reporters. In most instances, the public never knew any deal had been cut.[9]

But in Cleveland's day this was how the system worked. Corruption was simply part of the political equation in nineteenth-century America. As muckraking journalist Lincoln Steffens observed in *The Shame of the Cities*, politics in England is a sport, in Germany a profession, but in the United States, "politics is business." Large corporations had their hand in politics on every level, both legally and illegally, working hand-in-hand with political machines like Tammany Hall. After Harrison's close victory in 1888, a race in which he lost the popular vote, the president-elect remarked to friends, "Providence has given us the victory." But such high-minded rhetoric did not amuse Pennsylvania Boss Matt Quay. "Think of the man," he said. "He ought to know that providence hadn't a damn thing to do with it." Harrison, Quay noted, never knew "how close a number of men were compelled to approach the gates of the penitentiary to make him president."[10]

Cleveland, however, would not tolerate any deal making. "I will make no pledges. I will consent to none made for me," he told his campaign managers. "If I cannot go into the White House unpledged, I will not go at all." He also let it be known that if any pledges were made in his name, without his consent, he would disregard them. With such tough talk, Cleveland had stepped onto new ground. It was through "a series of improbabilities," writes Richard Hofstadter, "that a man of Cleveland's caliber became president in the Gilded Age." And when he became president, he vowed to clean up the corrupt system – and did, unlike his predecessors. He made good on his threat, ignoring any deal and promise made on his behalf.[11]

Cleveland also showed remarkable character when it came to the political issues facing the people. Time and again he stood on principle no matter the political consequences. He would rather lose an election than sacrifice his values, he often told his aides. He hated political expediency, which is doing things for purely electoral reasons, and loathed anyone who stooped to that level.

He absolutely would not triangulate on policy matters, the practice of taking up an opponent's issue to rob him of it. Cleveland faced a strong third-party candidate in his first White House run in 1884, Ben Butler of the Greenback Party, who bid for some of the same support, especially from Tammany Hall, run by John Kelly. To undercut Butler, campaign managers floated the idea that Cleveland could co-opt several issues from him, most importantly the imposition of inflationary currency to help debtors, and then kowtow to Kelly in order to keep Tammany off his back. But Cleveland did not think or act in such a politically calculated manner. Not in the slightest. He stuck to his Democratic principles no matter the political cost. To Daniel Lamont, his close personal aide and one of the campaign's managers, he wrote that he had no intention of bowing to either Butler or Kelly. "Now this is for you privately. I want to tell you how I feel. I had rather be beaten in this race than to truckle to Butler or Kelly. I don't want any pledge made for me that will violate my profession or betray and deceive the good people who believe in me." Tammany eventually supported Cleveland, albeit reluctantly, which had the effect of undercutting Butler's candidacy, making it a non-factor.[12]

While president in 1887, Cleveland decided to make his stand on the tariff issue, one of the hottest political topics of the era, in order to uphold the promises he made on the campaign trail to reduce the high rates that had been in place for nearly 30 years. In December of that year, he sent Congress his annual message centered solely on the tariff, an unheard-of tactic. He wanted to focus the nation's attention on the reduction of duties and then push through a tax cut bill in the spring of 1888. Coming as it did in an election year, his aides tried to persuade him to tone down his effort for the campaign. But he would hear none of it. "I would stultify myself if I failed to let the message go forward from any fear that it might affect my election," he told them. "What's the use of being reelected unless you stand for something?" Later in the election year of 1888, the bill was defeated in the Senate, and Cleveland was defeated in November. But he stood his ground and remained true to his principles.[13]

WORK ETHIC

Grover Cleveland's work ethic was legendary. White House staff, politicians from both parties, reporters, and friends marveled at how hard he labored each and every day. He often worked in his upstairs office until 2:00 a.m. or later and was usually back at it by 8:00 a.m. It was not unusual for him to spend "fifteen to eighteen hours out of the twenty-four" hard at work, wrote O. O. Stealy, the Washington correspondent for the *Louisville Courier-Journal*. Walter H. Page, a reporter from North Carolina, noted that the president "rises early and works late and does not waste his time – all because his time is now not his own but the Republic's, whose most honored servant he is." Often after finishing a long day of laborious work, he would shove back from his desk and tell his private secretary, Dan Lamont, "Well, I guess we'll quit and call it half a day." According to Allan Nevins, Cleveland "probably worked longer hours, day after day, than any other President since James K. Polk, who had worked himself to death."[14]

Cleveland had complete allegiance to the people and believed it his solemn duty to work hard on their behalf. His speeches and writings are littered with references to the people – how he did not want to disappoint them and hoped he could serve them effectively. Thomas F. Pendel, who served as doorkeeper of the White House in every administration from Abraham Lincoln to Theodore Roosevelt, remarked in his memoir that Cleveland "was a very hard worker—the hardest working president I ever saw in my life." White House usher Ike Hoover observed Cleveland's work ethic during his second term. Hoover served every administration from Benjamin Harrison to Franklin Roosevelt and wrote that Cleveland was "the most laborious of all the presidents under whom I have served."[15]

As a chief executive, one aspect of duty is to decide which bills to approve and which to reject. While modern-day presidents and politicians generally never read bills before voting on or signing them, usually passing off laborious work to aides, Cleveland, citing duty, took on the load himself. And he was meticulous in his detail. If bills had been sloppily written, he would not sign them. As governor he once angered a young legislator named Theodore Roosevelt by threatening to veto his set of municipal reform bills because they were carelessly drafted. Upon hearing of the threatened vetoes, Roosevelt demanded a meeting with Cleveland, and when he arrived in the governor's office burst out, "You must not veto those bills. You cannot. You shall not ... I won't have it!" Cleveland, slamming his fist down on his desk, shot back, "Mr. Roosevelt, I am going to veto those bills!" And he did. Once a bill had been passed and sent to him, observed David S. Barry, a political reporter and one-time sergeant-at-arms for the US Senate, Cleveland "took off his coat, hung it on the back of a chair, and sat down to burn the midnight oil in reading the bills and personally setting forth his endorsement or his opposition thereto."[16]

Other than the occasional vacation, which usually never lasted more than a week, Cleveland rarely enjoyed leisure activities. Professional baseball was an up–and-coming sport in the late nineteenth century, and he was very fond of it. He once hosted the Chicago White Stockings (now the Chicago Cubs) at the White House. When invited to the ballpark to watch an upcoming game, Cleveland respectfully declined. "No, thank you," he told manager Cap Anson. "What do you think the American people would think of me if I wasted my time going to a ball game?"[17]

Cleveland also sought to change the decorum of the presidency, as Thomas Jefferson had when he entered the White House in 1801. In Jefferson's opinion the office had already taken on the style of a monarch. His predecessor, John Adams, had even wanted to give the president a title befitting that of a king: "His Highness the President of the United States and Defender of the Rights of the Same." Adams loved the trappings of high office. Wearing an expensive suit that included an elegant sword, he'd arrived at his inaugural ceremony in a fancy carriage pulled by a fine team of white horses. By contrast, Jefferson had worn a simple suit with shoes that laced rather than buckled – which he felt was too aristocratic – and walked to the Capitol for his inauguration rather than in a horse-drawn carriage. Residing in the mansion, he opened the door himself when someone knocked, even in his sleep attire, and removed the large rectangular dining table in favor of a circular one so that everyone present would be considered equal. He also served his guests personally, rather than have a servant do it.

Like Jefferson, Cleveland also had a lavish predecessor in Chester A. Arthur, who at the time would have been called a "dandy." Arthur loved the finer things in life, like fancy clothes, fine furniture, silver utensils, and the most expensive wines. Upon winning the vice presidency in 1880, he went on a shopping spree at Brooks Brothers, spending hundreds of dollars on new clothes. After becoming president with the tragic assassination of James A. Garfield, he completely redecorated the White House because he felt it had become too drab and dreary, even selling off much of the furnishings. He then filled the mansion with new furniture and also new employees – butlers, personal servants, valets, and even a French chef. When Mrs. James G. Blaine dined one evening with President Arthur, she wrote later that the "dinner was extremely elegant," with "hardly a trace of the old White House taint being perceptible anywhere." The "flowers, the silver, the attendants, all showing the latest style and an abandon in expense and taste."[18]

Cleveland followed in Jefferson's footsteps. He did not like the pomp and pageantry of any public position, what he once termed the "purely ornamental part of the office." The White House paymaster, Colonel W. H. Crook, wrote that Cleveland "was a plain, simple man, who had no desire to make himself prominent" with lavish events. He spent the "better part of each night over his desk" and generally kept himself "so deeply occupied that he could not see any one except on official business." From his first days in the White House, Crook noted that he "felt that the glitter of official life was distasteful to Mr. Cleveland. He was a man who believed that he had work to accomplish, and that work was a serious matter which must be attended to, and with which nothing must interfere." Cleveland was married during his first term, in a ceremony in the White House, and according to Crook, Cleveland worked "as hard as he ever did in his life" on the day of his wedding. He "worked harder, and kept longer hours than any other president we have ever had."[19]

Since the presidency had been greatly strengthened under Lincoln, Cleveland, like Jefferson, opposed its evolution into that of a monarchy, particularly where appearance was concerned. He dispensed with as much luxury as possible, dismissing all of Arthur's servants, even the fancy French chef. Ike Hoover witnessed Cleveland's cuts to the White

House staff. The president dismissed "practically all of the domestic help; had a cyclone struck this portion of the establishment, it could not have been swept cleaner." Hoover noted that more "changes were made during the first two or three days of this administration than at any other time the oldest employee can remember."[20]

Even though he loved to fish on his days off, Cleveland refused to use the presidential yacht, the *Dispatch*. His executive staff was reduced to an almost nonexistent level, consisting of just a handful of men. If an aide were not available, Cleveland answered the recently installed White House telephone himself. To pay White House bills, he personally wrote out the checks. The American people had not seen such a president since the days of Jefferson.

CLEAN GOVERNMENT

Nineteenth-century politics was a dirty affair, an era full of scandal and corruption on a scale that is hard for modern Americans to fathom. Dens of corruption, known as rings, littered the cities of the great industrial North. Perhaps the most infamous, the Tweed Ring of New York City, stole an incalculable amount of public money, with some estimates as high as $200 million. The Tweed Ring and the superfluous corruption are very accurately portrayed in the Martin Scorsese film *Gangs of New York*.

One of the worst Tweed scandals concerned the construction of a new county courthouse in New York City, originally budgeted at $250,000, a mighty sum in 1862, but by the time it was finished a decade later, taxpayers had been bilked for $14 million, most of it finding its way into the pockets of the Tweed Ring. The amount of money skimmed by the Ring on the courthouse construction, according to scholar Edwin Burrows and journalist Mike Wallace, equaled "four times as much as the Houses of Parliament and twice the price of Alaska."[21]

Roy Morris Jr., in *Fraud of the Century: Rutherford B. Hayes, Samuel Tilden, and the Stolen Election of 1876*, relates a story about how Tweed's corruption actually worked. An electrician, who wanted to install fire alarms in the new courthouse building, submitted a high bid for the sum of $60,000. Boss Tweed responded to his request by asking, "If we get you a contract for $450,000, will you give us $225,000?" This was the Tweed machine in action, with surcharges to the city ranging from 10 to 85 percent. Money stolen from public treasuries was then used to fund the political machine – to pay its members, bribe politicians, hire workers, buy votes, and, ultimately, to stay in power, thereby allowing the ring to maintain its position and the theft to continue. The cycle continued in perpetuity it seemed. Very few public officials dared to take on the rings for fear of being ground down by their power and might. Many just went along and reaped the rotten, though eventually welcomed, rewards.[22]

Cleveland's own hometown of Buffalo was no island oasis in this vast sea of theft. Being in the hands of Republicans a majority of the time, it was as corrupt and inefficient as any northern city. But Democrats were by no means immune to scandal. The municipal government had come under the influence of an "aldermanic ring," led by dishonest, thieving politicians from both parties. Mayors, regardless of party, were generally "yes men" who allowed the various city departments to grow tremendously, likely due to graft and corruption, but most probably because the mayor was also part of the gang. Many of the town's citizens, particularly the more affluent who paid the highest taxes, wanted the ring cleaned up and asked Grover Cleveland to run for mayor in 1881.[23]

That autumn, he accepted the nomination and spoke to an assembly of Democrats to outline the philosophy that would govern his administration, placing a strong emphasis on fiscal conservatism. "I believe that much can be done to relieve our citizens from their present load of taxation, and that a more rigid scrutiny of all public expenditures will result in a great savings to the community. I also believe that some extravagance in our city government may be corrected without injury to the public service." Government officials should treat the people's money as honestly as they did their own, he contended. "There is, or there should be, no reason why the affairs of our city should not be managed with the same care and the same economy as private interests. And when we consider that public officials are the trustees of the people, and hold their places and exercise their powers for the benefit of the people, there should be no higher inducement to a faithful and honest discharge of public duty."[24]

Throughout the brief fall campaign, he echoed similar themes, vowing to clean up the corruption and bring fiscal sanity to City Hall. He spoke to people wherever he found them, even in bars, where he once addressed patrons standing atop tables. "We believe in the principle of economy of the people's money," he told one crowd, "and that when a man in office lays out a dollar in extravagance, he acts immorally by the people." There would be no waste, fraud, abuse, or special earmarks when he ran the mayor's office. "A Democratic thief is as bad as a Republican thief," he told another group. "Why shouldn't public interests be conducted in the same excellent manner as private interests?" He also echoed Thomas Jefferson's famous "tree of liberty" theme. "It is a good thing for the people now and then to rise up and let the officeholders know they are responsible to the masses."[25]

The people enthusiastically responded to his message and gave him an overwhelming victory at the polls. Wasting no time, on his first day in office he sent a written message to the city's Common Council, one that concentrated heavily on fiscal responsibility. "We hold the money of the people in our hands to be used for their purposes and to further their interests as members of the municipality," he told the members. When "any part of the funds which the taxpayers have thus entrusted to us is diverted to other purposes, or when, by design or neglect, we allow a greater sum to be applied to any municipal purpose than is necessary, we have, to that extent, violated our duty." To the new mayor, there could be "no difference in his duties and obligations, whether a person is entrusted with the money of one man or many. And yet it sometimes appears as though the officeholder assumes that a different rule of fidelity prevails between him and the taxpayers than that which should regulate his conduct when, as an individual, he holds the money of his neighbor."[26]

Mayor Cleveland took on the ring when no one else would. In his boldest move, he vetoed a street sweeping contract rife with corruption and kickbacks. The issue concerned a five-year agreement the city had awarded to a company to clean the streets. The business in question, owned by George Talbot, had previously done business with the city and submitted a bid of $422,500 for the contract. The council approved it by a vote of fifteen to eleven, even though the bid was $100,000 more than the lowest proposal. In fact, *five* companies submitted lower bids. Furthermore, the council's appropriation was $50,000 *higher* than the original bid. Cleveland quickly suspected that palms had been greased. The extra funds had to be a kickback.[27]

Cleveland immediately vetoed the bill and ripped into the members for such outrageous behavior. "This is a time for plain speech," he told the council in his veto message. The bill was nothing more than the "culmination of a most barefaced, impudent, and shameless scheme to betray the interests of the people and worse ... to squander the public money." He warned the members to be mindful of "influences, both in and about your honorable body, which it behooves every honest man to watch and avoid with the greatest care." When it came to being good public stewards, there could be "no middle ground. Those who are not for the people either in or out of your honorable body are against them and should be treated accordingly." The corrupt council vowed to override the veto, especially after Cleveland's tongue-lashing message hit the press. But the override attempt failed.

Talbot and Cleveland were actually acquaintances, as the former had been a client in the mayor's old law firm. But that didn't matter to Mayor Cleveland. Afterward, he explained the matter to Talbot. "This is neither a personal nor a legal matter. While I was your attorney I was loyal to your interests. Now the people are my clients, and I must be loyal to them." He would not reward personal friends out of the public treasury, which was commonplace in the North at that time. He served the people and no one else. "I only did my public duty," he told fellow Buffalonian Arthur S. Bissell after the veto. The following day, the *Courier* ran the headline "A Victory for the People." As for the present council, noted the paper, "Mayor Cleveland has turned out the lights and torn off all disguises."[28]

During his one year in office, he saved the citizens of Buffalo more than a million dollars, big money in those days. By tackling corruption head-on and dressing down members of the City Council for tolerating it, Cleveland impressed party officials across the state. The boldness of his crusade enthralled western New Yorkers and launched his successful campaign for governor in 1882.

As governor he took on Tammany Hall, the great Democratic political machine, and, as a former home of the Tweed Ring, a major and efficient engine of corruption. No one in New York City politics in the late nineteenth century dared trifle with Tammany, but Cleveland possessed no fear. He dismissed corrupt officials connected to the machine, signed reform bills, cut the size of government, and publicly exposed Tammany's vice. From the first moment he arrived in Albany, "Tammany hated Cleveland with a sleepless vindictiveness," noted biographer Allan Nevins.[29]

In his capacity as New York's chief executive officer, Cleveland was responsible for upholding and maintaining the state's election laws. He had campaigned on a pledge to preserve clean elections, leaving them "uncontaminated and fairly conducted." In November 1883, just before the annual legislative elections, he issued a proclamation for state and local officials to enforce "laws relating to bribery and corruption at elections." A clean electoral process, he reminded public officials, "is absolutely the foundation upon which our institutions rest." Elections "should be fairly expressed and honestly regarded. Without this, our system is a sham and a contrivance, which it is brazen effrontery to call a republican form of government." So the governor called on "all district attorneys within this state, and all sheriffs and peace officers and others having in charge the execution of the laws to exercise the utmost diligence in the discovery and punishment of violations of the statutes referred to, and they are admonished that neglect of duty in this regard will be promptly dealt with." Despite the dirtiness of the era's politics, Cleveland believed the electoral process, as importantly as political offices, should be free from corruption. And he vowed to hold accountable public servants who failed to do their duty.[30]

Because he worked hard on behalf of the people and was honest to a fault, Cleveland expected those serving under him in the government to do likewise. He loathed lazy, incompetent bureaucrats and vowed to fire anyone who did not give the taxpayers an honest day's work for an honest day's wage. As mayor, Cleveland criticized the practice of city offices closing "at the early hour in the day, which seems now to be regarded as the limit of a day's work." The taxpayers paid the salaries and wages of city employees and were entitled "to a fair day's work."[31]

He also did not want government employees involved in politics, which was the custom of the time. During his first presidential campaign, he swore to the people that "public departments will not be filled with those who conceive it to be their first duty to aid the party to which they owe their places, instead of rendering patient and honest return to the people." When he became president, he did not change his mind or his stance, as many modern presidents do. "I insist upon officeholders ... attending to the duties of their offices and not interfering improperly with the political actions of others," he wrote to a friend during his first presidential term.[32]

In the nineteenth century there was no law preventing bureaucrats from being involved in political campaigns, so the political party holding the presidency routinely mobilized the entirety of the governmental workforce to participate in a variety of campaign activities, such as public speaking, distributing pamphlets, and raising funds. In the pre–civil service days, most federal workers owed their jobs to presidential appointment, so bureaucrats had a stake in the outcome of the election. If the other party prevailed, they would find themselves out of a job.

President Cleveland ended that practice, just as he'd promised voters he would, with an executive order on July 14, 1886, to "warn all subordinates" in the federal government "against the use of their official positions in attempts to control political movements in their localities." Public officials "are the agents of the people, not their masters" and should avoid any "display of obtrusive partisanship." Those who hold public office have no right to "dictate the political action of their party associates or to throttle freedom of action within party lines." Furthermore, they could not engage in the "manipulation of political primary meetings and nominating conventions." However, their rights as voting citizens would not be infringed upon. But when two officials decided to test his resolve, both were fired.[33]

In Cleveland's day, before the completion of civil service reform, presidents appointed tens of thousands of people to offices across the country, even down to the local postmasters in the smallest towns. When the opposing party won the White House, the entire government changed hands, so the new president faced a barrage of office seekers who filled the White House halls, as well as the lawn, hoping to get an interview and a job offer. The president also relied on members of Congress and others – party members, friends, and friends of friends – to recommend appointees, as the president could not hope to know enough qualified people in every state in America. And if that appointment did not turn out to be sound, Cleveland's wrath would most assuredly be felt.

One poor fellow felt the full brunt of Cleveland's hostility by recommending someone for appointment who turned out to be unreliable. After writing a letter to the president confessing the error of his recommendation, Cleveland responded by accusing him of committing an unpardonable crime, and even treason, which should be punished with a jail sentence:

> I have read your letter ... with amazement and indignation. There is but one mitigation to the perfidy which your letter discloses and that is found in the fact

that you confess your share in it. I don't know whether you are a Democrat or not; but if you are, the crime which you confess is the more unpardonable. The idea that this administration, pledged to give the people better government and better officers, and engaged in a hand-to-hand fight with the base elements of both parties, should be betrayed by those who ought to be worthy of implicit trust, is atrocious; and such treason to the people and the party ought to be punished by imprisonment.

Your confession comes too late to be of immediate use to the public service; and I can only say that while this is not the first time I have been deceived and tricked by lying and treacherous representations, you are the first one that has so frankly owned his grievous fault. If any comfort is to be extracted from this assurance you are welcome to it.[34]

Throughout his two-term presidency, unworthy officials were removed from service regardless of party affiliation, while vice and corruption were both stamped out. Cleveland earned praise from the *New York World* newspaper for the "destroyed nests of corruption in the Navy Department, the Treasury, the Indian Bureau, the Land Office, the Coast Survey, and the War Department."[35]

The American people, fed up with all the corruption in government, wanted a strong president with the courage and character to clean it up. When he endorsed Cleveland for president in 1884, Joseph Pulitzer, in his *New York World* paper, did so for four reasons: "1. He is an honest man. 2. He is an honest man. 3. He is an honest man. 4. He is an honest man." Cleveland had pledged to the people he would provide good government, and he worked hard each and every day to see that they had it.[36]

OPENNESS AND TRANSPARENCY

In his life of public service, Grover Cleveland maintained one of the most open governments in history. As president, Cleveland made himself available to the general public. He held open houses two days a week, allowing citizens to walk in and shake his hand, as well as discuss political matters with him. He once told George F. Parker, his secretary, that it was "one of the characteristic features of our institutions that any person, young or old, rich or poor, white or black, known or obscure, could, if even decently clad, not only see the man who, for the time, was the head of his country's management, but that he could speak to him upon any question in which he had a peculiar interest."[37]

Even in the White House, if one knocked on the front door it was not unusual to be received by Cleveland himself, the last president to engage in the practice. During Cleveland's residence, fences did not surround the executive mansion, nor were there any guard shacks, Secret Service agents trolling about, or security at the entrances to the building. All one had to do was walk up to the White House and knock on the door to see the president, who would generally listen to concerns or desires, if he had the time.[38]

As governor, Cleveland also had a very open, transparent, and accessible government. In a manner strikingly Jacksonian, his first official act was to open the mansion to all visitors. His executive offices at the state capitol were also open to any who desired to call upon him "without the intermediary services of a secretary or a clerk," noted his aide William Hudson. Lt. Governor David B. Hill remarked that the policy resembled "a town meeting. The governor might just as well place his desk on the grass in front of the Capitol." Hill hated the idea, believing it a "waste of energy" that "must be stopped." Cleveland later altered the policy when he saw how much time he needed to conduct the state's business but, while governor, wrote Hudson, "access to him was easy." A reporter from the *New York Herald* also acknowledged the difference in accessibility. "The formalities surrounding a visit to the governor, so annoying under former administrations, are entirely absent now. Little trouble is experienced by the humblest citizen in having an interview with the governor of the state."[39]

Cleveland had just one instance of real governmental secrecy, in his second term as president. In 1893, while battling a severe economic depression, a calamity perhaps second only to the Great Depression in severity, he hid cancer surgery from the public. After finding a rough spot on the roof of his mouth, Cleveland had doctors examine him. Their determination was that it was a cancerous growth that needed to be removed as soon as possible, along with part of his upper jaw, in order to ensure his future health.

Normally, having an operation of that magnitude would be public knowledge. However, the economic situation was precarious. The problem concerned the nation's monetary policy and a possible presidential succession. Cleveland believed in maintaining the gold standard at all costs, which at the time was under threat, while his vice president, Adlai Stevenson, favored the free and unlimited coinage of silver. The president feared that if word surfaced that he was undergoing a perilous surgery and could possibly die, a situation that would leave the nation's economic fate in the hands of the Silverite Stevenson, panic might grip the business community and the markets. The nation's fragile economic situation, which he was in the process of trying to stabilize, might collapse. Fortunately, Cleveland survived the surgery and had no further bouts with cancer. Yet while the true story hit the press, the White House denied it, telling reporters that the president had some dental work done. Though it might have gone against his Jeffersonian instincts, Cleveland felt that the nation's economic well-being, and with it that of the people, was more important.

RETIREMENT

Unlike modern presidents, who make tons of money and stay in the political arena by campaigning for their fellow party members, after he retired Cleveland would not campaign for Democratic candidates, refusing on many occasions to take part. As the only living Democratic president, many party members looked to Cleveland for leadership, especially during his first retirement in 1889. Though he was out of power, he still remained the top Democrat in the country. The former president found himself bombarded with letters from across the country for advice about how best to defend party principles and attack the Republicans. "I find it very hard to shake off the results of my official incumbency," he wrote his friend William Vilas. "It takes much of my time to answer letters of all sorts, and it really seems sometimes as though the people did not appreciate that I was no longer president. Everybody is very kind to me, but the pressing invitations to go to all sorts of places embarrass me a good deal, for I feel that I must work or be ready to work as it comes along. I am very pleasantly situated professionally and think I shall gradually get on."[40]

During his retirement, the popular former president was asked to speak on behalf of Democratic candidates. But he was simply not up to the task, mostly because such an undertaking would take up time he wanted to devote to work and family – not to mention the fact that he did not particularly like making public speeches. His letters of regret were usually lighthearted. "There are very few things I would not do for you and the others for whom you speak," he wrote to Governor William E. Russell of Massachusetts. "I want to avoid all the speechmaking possible, for in the first place I do not think I am very good at it, and secondly, during my vacation I am such a vagabond and lazy good-for-nothing that I find any mental exercise a great effort." To another friend he wrote that he was "in a miserable condition," a "private citizen without political ambition trying to do private work and yet pulled and hauled and importuned daily and hourly to do things in a public and semi-public way which are hard and distasteful to me." The flood of requests was "as wearing and perplexing as it was to refuse applications for office at Washington." To him, ex-presidents were simply private citizens and should remain as such.[41]

Grover Cleveland had among the most honest and ethical administrations in history. Whether during his stint as mayor, governor, or president, he was never called upon to explain scandals to the public, which have plagued so many presidential administrations, because there were none. He prided himself in selecting the most competent public officials. He was a good judge of character and made sound appointments. And those who proved to be otherwise were summarily dismissed from service. He kept his pledge to provide the people with good government.

Endnotes

1   John C. Calhoun to George McDuffie, December 4, 1843, in Wilson, ed., *The Essential Calhoun*, 345.

2   Merrill, 24, 54; Muzzey, 311.

3   Lewis Gould, *Grand Old Party: A History of the Republicans* (New York: Random House, 2003), 100.

4   Cleveland to Charles W. Goodyear, July 23, 1884, Nevins, *Letters*, 37.

5   A new book focused entirely on this story was published in 2011 and authored by Charles Lachman, entitled *A Secret Life: The Lies and Scandals of President Grover Cleveland* (New York: Skyhorse Publishing). In the book, Lachman, the executive producer of the television tabloid *Inside Edition*, takes Halpin's side and makes the shocking claim that Cleveland raped her. His evidence is an affidavit produced by Halpin. Yet her testimony was taken, not at the time of the incident, but just weeks before the 1884 presidential election, and then sent out to *Republican* newspapers in an "October Surprise." Lachman's argument is so completely ridiculous that it is not worthy of any prominence other than this endnote.

6   Cleveland to Daniel N. Lockwood, July 31, 1884, Nevins, *Letters*, 38–9.

7   William C. Hudson, *Random Recollections of an Old Political Reporter* (New York: Cupples and Leon Company, 1911), 184-185.

8   Bruce Chadwick, *Lincoln for President: An Unlikely Candidate, An Audacious Strategy, and the Victory No One Saw Coming* (Naperville, Il: Source Books, 2009), 82-4; Richard Hofstadter, *The American Political Tradition: And the Men Who Made It* (New York, Vintage Books, 1948), 223.

9   Details of the meeting can be found in Thomas C. Platt, *The Autobiography of Thomas Collier Platt* (New York: B. W. Dodge & Company, 1910), 126-132. Platt was in attendance at the meeting to speak for Conkling. Also see Kenneth C. Ackerman, *Dark Horse: The Surprise Election and Political Murder of President James A. Garfield* (New York: Da Capo Press, 2004), 174–5.

10   Lincoln Steffens, *The Shame of the Cities* (New York: McClure, Phillips & Co., 1904), 6-7; Hofstadter, *American Political Tradition*, 223.

11   Hudson, 240; Hofstadter, *American Political Tradition*, 234.

12   Cleveland to George W. Curtis, October 24, 1884 and Cleveland to Daniel Lamont, August 11, 1884, Nevins, *Letters*, 47, 40.

13   Brodsky, 207-8.

14   Stealy, 29; Hendrick, *The Life and Letters of Walter H. Page*, 41; Nevins, *Cleveland*, 127, 214.

15   Thomas Pendel, *Thirty-Six Years in the White House: A Memoir of the White House Doorkeeper from Lincoln to Roosevelt* (Washington: The Neal Publishing Company, 1902), 148; Irwin Hood Hoover, *Forty-Two Years in the White House* (Boston: Houghton Mifflin Company, 1934), 13.

16   Hudson, 148-9; David Barry, *Forty Years in Washington* (Boston: Little, Brown, and Company, 1924), 167.

17   Henry Graff, *Grover Cleveland* (New York: Times Books, 2002), 75.

18   Mrs. James G. Blaine to M., March 13, 1882, *Letters of Mrs. James G. Blaine*, edited by Harriet S. Blaine Beale, 2 volumes. (New York: Duffield and Company, 1908), II, 4-5.

19   Crook, 172-4, 176, 179, 188.

20   Ike Hoover, 12.

21   Roy Morris Jr., *Fraud of the Century: Rutherford B. Hayes, Samuel Tilden, and the Stolen Election of 1876* (New York: Simon and Schuster, 2003), 100; Edwin G. Burrows and Mike Wallace, *Gotham: A History of New York City to 1898* (New York: Oxford University Press, 1999), 1009.

22   Morris, *Fraud*, 100; Burrows and Wallace, 1009.

23   Nevins, *Cleveland*, 79.

24   Cleveland, Speech Accepting Nomination for Mayor before City Convention in Buffalo, October 25, 1881, Parker, *Writings and Speeches*, 1-2.

25   Nevins, *Cleveland*, 82-3; *Buffalo Daily Courier*, October 26, 1881 and November 5, 1881.

26   Cleveland, Mayoral Message, January 2, 1882, Parker, *Writings and Speeches*, 28-30.

27   Armitage, 103, 105.

28   *Ibid.*, 104-5, 109; *Buffalo Daily Courier*, June 27, 1882.

29   Nevins, *Cleveland*, 135-6.

30   Cleveland, Proclamation against the Violation of Laws Governing Elections, *Public Papers of Grover Cleveland, Governor, 1883*-1884, 2 volumes. (Albany: Argus Company, Printers, 1883), I, 149-50.

31   Cleveland, Mayoral Message, January 2, 1882, Parker, *Writings and Speeches*, 28-30.

32   Cleveland, Letter Accepting Nomination for President, August 18, 1884, Parker, *Writings and Speeches*, 9-13; Cleveland to John Temple Graves, July 30, 1887, Nevins, *Letters*, 147.

33   Cleveland, Executive Order, July 14, 1886, in Grover Cleveland Presidential Papers, The American Presidency Project, University of California at Santa Barbara, www.presidency.ucsb.edu.

34   Cleveland to A. Bush, August 1, 1885, Nevins, *Letters*, 69-70.

35   *New York World*, August 13, 1885, as quoted in Nevins, *Cleveland*, 215.

36   Nevins, *Cleveland*, 4.

37   Parker, *Recollections*, 112.

38   Graff, 74-75; Jeffers, 137; Richard V. Oulahan, "Presidents & Publicity," 15-16, unpublished book manuscript, located in the Richard V. Oulahan Papers, Herbert Hoover Presidential Library, West Branch, Iowa. Oulahan served as an assistant reporter during Cleveland's second term.

39   Hudson, 138; *New York Herald*, January 4, 1883.

40   Cleveland to Vilas, September 15, 1889, Nevins, *Letters*, 210-11.

41   Cleveland to William E. Russell, June 9, 1891, Nevins, *Letters*, 256; Cleveland to L. Clarke Davis, March 9, 1891, *Ibid.*, 249-50.

Chapter 3

BUSINESSMAN'S PRESIDENT OR MAN OF THE PEOPLE?

"To preserve the faith of the nation by an exact discharge of its debts and contracts, expend the public money with the same care and economy we would practice with our own, and impose on our citizens no unnecessary burden... are the landmarks by which we are to guide ourselves in all our proceedings."

—President Thomas Jefferson,
Second Annual Message to Congress, December 15, 1802

"It is the duty of those serving the people in public place to closely limit public expenditures to the actual needs of the government economically administered, and our system of revenue shall be so adjusted as to relieve the people of unnecessary taxation ... preventing the accumulation of a surplus in the Treasury to tempt extravagance and waste."

—President Grover Cleveland,
First Inaugural Address, March 4, 1885.

Throughout the vast historical literature of the Gilded Age, scholars have repeatedly, and unfairly, branded Grover Cleveland an exclusive champion of the business interests. They say he was in the pockets of Wall Street and the big banks, and that he did not hold the lower classes in high regard. But these attacks are one of the most erroneous ascertains in academia. Cleveland did not believe in government assistance for any group, rich or poor, because such aid from Washington would only build dependence on government and unjustly rob taxpayers of the fruit of their labor, a violation of his cherished Jeffersonian ideology.

GOVERNMENT PATERNALISM

Throughout America's political and constitutional history, a basic question routinely arises: What role should the government play in the everyday lives of ordinary citizens? There have been numerous answers.

For the emerging progressives of Cleveland's day, it was thought that perhaps the government should play a more active role in the lives of the people. For Jeffersonians, the government has no authority to get involved in areas outside its limited, constitutional role and should never take a position as a custodian. The people are free to pursue their own dreams without government interference, to rise as high and as far as their God-given talent, abilities, and determination will carry them. As President Jefferson wrote in 1802, "If we can but prevent the government from wasting the labours of the people, under the pretence [sic] of taking care of them, they must become happy."[1]

Cleveland, as a strong Jeffersonian, rightly understood that the government should never interfere in the free market nor meddle in the lives of the people. By keeping Washington's hands out of private matters, the people could easily ascend the social ladder with desire, determination, discipline, hard work, and thrift, just as he, and many others like him, had done. Handouts and the subsequent laziness that comes with a slothful lifestyle would only result in entrapment at the bottom, thereby breeding more dependence on the government. It was a cycle that would never be broken, and history has proven Cleveland right.

As president, Grover Cleveland would not allow the government to assume the role of parent for either the rich or the poor. But in the latter part of the nineteenth century, paternalistic ideas, though rare, were slowly beginning to emerge and become more prevalent, mainly from the mouths of Republicans. James A. Garfield, elected president in 1880, was described by the *Boston Herald* as the representative of the "liberal and progressive wing of the party," though we have no way of knowing if he would have governed that way or not, since he served but two hundred days in office before succumbing to the assassin's bullet of Charles Guiteau.[2]

President Rutherford B. Hayes sought federal aid for public education, and after leaving office he became what amounted to a socialist, pondering "how to secure a more equal distribution of property among the people." He advocated crippling inheritance taxes and government support for the elderly. Hayes's plan called for inheritance to be capped at $500,000. All inherited wealth of more than half a million dollars would be confiscated by the government to distribute to those less fortunate.[3]

Jacob Coxey, a wealthy businessman who led an "army" of unemployed men from Ohio to Washington D.C. during the Panic of 1893, lobbied Congress to issue $500 million in new paper currency to spend on public works, a precursor to FDR's New Deal of the 1930s. At the time, the entire federal budget was less than $500 million. But the Jeffersonian Democratic Congress never seriously considered it.[4]

No such ideas or notions ever came from Grover Cleveland. "It is the duty of those serving the people in public place to closely limit public expenditures to the actual needs of the government economically administered," he said in his first presidential inaugural address in 1885, and "our system of revenue shall be so adjusted as to relieve the people of unnecessary taxation ... preventing the accumulation of a surplus in the Treasury to tempt extravagance and waste." Upon winning the 1892 nomination for a second attempt at a second presidential term, Cleveland wrote in his letter of acceptance, "Paternalism in government finds no approval in the creed of Democracy. It is a symptom of misrule, whether it is manifested in unauthorized gifts or by an unwarranted control of personal and family affairs." There would be no handouts or government intrusion of any kind under his leadership.[5]

COMBATING HANDOUTS TO THE POOR

During the eight years of a Cleveland administration, whenever Congress decided to get generous with other people's money, the president struck it down with his veto pen. During the late 1880s, a severe drought struck Texas. Without a federal disaster relief agency in those days, Congress sought to help in its own way. During the first term, in February 1887, federal legislators appropriated $10,000 to buy seed to distribute to suffering farmers. President Cleveland, without hesitation, vetoed the bill, returning it to Congress with one of his most famous declarations:

I can find no warrant for such an appropriation in the Constitution, and I do not believe that the power and duty of the general government ought to be extended to the relief of individual suffering, which is in no manner properly related to the public service or benefit. A prevalent tendency to disregard the limited mission of this power and duty should, I think, be steadfastly resisted, to the end that the lesson should be constantly enforced that though the people support the government the government should not support the people.

The friendliness and charity of our countrymen can always be relied upon to relieve their fellow-citizens in misfortune. This has been repeatedly and quite lately demonstrated. Federal aid in such cases encourages the expectation of paternal care on the part of the government and weakens the sturdiness of our national character, while it prevents the indulgence among our people of that kindly sentiment and conduct which strengthens the bonds of a common brotherhood.[6]

Jeffersonian Democrats across the country applauded Cleveland's veto. Texans, as exhibited in two of the state's major newspapers, also praised the president's action against the "seed bill," even though his decision directly affected their state. The *Houston Daily Post* called it "a very proper veto" of a bill that was "clearly unconstitutional." Crops fail in all parts of the country, noted the *Post*, and "it will not do to expect Uncle Sam to repair the damages wrought by nature." The *Dallas Morning News* noted that, although the veto might be "abrupt and ungracious" to some, it was "a truly exemplary act." The "Texas Democracy should look with peculiar pride and satisfaction upon an executive act indicating that the official head of the Democratic party of the country is disposed to assist a principle which they have so long cherished by laboring to redeem the national government, if possible, from the vice of paternalistic prodigality." Congress or the president should never "dream of thrusting the hand of government in the pockets of the people for either charity or robbery."[7]

Over the years, establishment historians have used this particular veto as evidence that Cleveland did not support farmers and the lower classes because of his favor toward the interests of business. But he supported the Constitution, first and foremost, over the interests of individual interest groups. He believed, as did all Jeffersonians, in "equal and exact justice to all men," that the government should see all people in the same light and should not divide them into classes. Furthermore, private charities and the goodness of the American people would be sufficient to take care of any needs among the populace. Government aid would only invite more government aid.

But lost in all the historical uproar was the result of Cleveland's request for private charitable help for Texas farmers. Some of the nation's leading newspapers issued calls for donations, as did Clara Barton, the president of the American Red Cross. In all, people across the nation raised money in excess of $100,000 for drought-stricken farmers in Texas, more than ten times what Congress sought to appropriate.[8]

Establishment historians of today, scholars who loathe Cleveland and Jeffersonians like him, are perplexed at such attitudes. For Jack Beatty, author of *The Age of Betrayal: The Triumph of Money in America, 1865–1900*, Cleveland's refusal of simple aid, such as seed to help farmers, raised important questions: "Why did the people support a government that on principle refused to support them, that wouldn't spend pennies to save farmers from ruin?" he asked. "Why return to office politicians like Cleveland, who vetoed three times as many bills in one term as all his predecessors combined? What had gone wrong with the Republican experiment in positive government for the country to settle for negative government?"[9]

What Beatty means by "positive government" would be, as Hamilton described it, a government of more energy, which Lincoln brought to fruition. As president, Lincoln had broken the old Jeffersonian mold and provided a new view of the role of government in the everyday lives of the people, once saying, "The legitimate object of government is to do for a community of people, whatever they need to have done, but cannot do, at all, or cannot so well do, for themselves—in their separate and individual capacities." But it was that attitude that Cleveland was trying to bury for good and most people, at least in the 1880s, sided with him.[10]

In addition to government charity, President Cleveland also weakened government paternalism in the area of pensions for Union soldiers, a vast federal program that had come to be what one scholar called the "first large-scale federal welfare system." And recall that only Union veterans could receive a pension from the federal government. No Confederate soldiers could claim any pensions. Yet Southerners had to pay the federal taxes that funded the pensions they were not allowed to receive.[11]

To receive a pension, the aged Union veterans of the great sectional conflict applied at the Federal Bureau of Pensions, which could either accept or reject the application based on the law. If the bureau rejected the application, the veteran or his dependent could appeal to representatives in Congress, who would then place a private pension bill on the floor to override the bureau's recommendation. This scheme had been in operation since the end of the Civil War and was popular enough that Congress had to set aside time each week, known as "pension day," to handle the barrage of these private pension bills. The situation was so bad that in the Forty-Ninth Congress, which sat during Cleveland's first two years as president from 1885 to 1887, forty percent of the bills passed by the House and fifty-five percent enacted in the Senate were private pension acts. The pension system had become just another way for Congress to dole out favors, pay campaign debts, and buy votes.[12]

Making matters worse, the pension system was rife with fraud and abuse, which the president had no patience for. A study of the pension system ordered by Cleveland found that one-fourth of all Union pensions were fraudulent. Given these unfortunate realities, President Cleveland set out to stop as much of it as he could, mainly with his veto pen. And he often displayed his distain in sarcastic veto messages. For example, in June 1886 he received a private pension bill for the relief of William Bishop, who was enrolled as a substitute soldier on March 25, 1865, just days before the war ended. During the next month he contracted the measles and was admitted to a hospital in Indianapolis. He did not return to duty until May 8 and was then mustered out of service on May 11. Cleveland pounced on the apparent giveaway. Despite Mr. Bishop's "brilliant service and terrific encounter with the measles," the president noted, the claim should be rejected, just as the pension bureau had recommended.[13]

In addition to measles, President Cleveland rejected pension claims by an applicant who "spent the most of his term of enlistment in desertion or in imprisonment as a punishment of that offense" and another who claimed "sore eyes among the results of diarrhea." Such shenanigans aggravated Cleveland as much as anything could. He continually lashed out at these repeated attempts to steal public funds. As he stated in one veto message, "I believe this claim for pension to be a fraud from beginning to end, and the effrontery with which it has been pushed shows the necessity of a careful examination of these cases," an investigation the hardworking president was always eager to conduct. After rejecting a widow's claim, submitted because her husband had died after falling off the roof in 1881, Cleveland summed up his feeling toward those pensions he believed were without merit. "It is not a pleasant thing to interfere in such a case," he wrote Congress in his veto message, "but we are dealing with pensions and not with gratuities." Cleveland showed courage and did what other presidents did not dare do by vetoing any payments to the multitude of soldiers who had "saved the Union." In all, he killed 228 of these private and mostly fraudulent pension acts.[14]

In an attempt to get around the president's persistence, Congress, in early 1887, decided to pass a new, more general pension law called the Dependent Pension Bill, which, unlike previous laws, established the precedent for providing pensions without regard to service-incurred disability. In other words, if a person had a disability and was unable to work, regardless of the cause of the handicap, and had served at least ninety days in the Union army, that person was entitled to a federal pension of twelve dollars a month. The proposal would also cover the veterans' dependents. But the bill was so bad and so obviously full of potential fraud that the *New York Times* referred to it as the "pauper pension bill."[15]

Cleveland, unhappy with the liberal requirements, summarily vetoed the bill as a raid on the treasury, stating that the pension list would cease to be "a roll of honor" but would include those "willing to be objects of simple charity." It was unfair to equate someone disabled by war to one who suffered from an unrelated disease, a farm accident, or the bottle. Those who incurred disabilities in any manner other than the war did not deserve a pension and would not receive one as long as Grover Cleveland was president.[16]

Cleveland believed he was simply doing his duty in upholding his constitutional oath of office. Historians, though, see something else altogether and have derided him for such acts they consider a callous disregard for the poor and working classes. Such criticism is so pervasive that it has come to define Cleveland in historical circles. Basic lectures in survey courses in American history all say that Cleveland was in the pockets of Wall Street, large corporations, and big banks, displaying a heartless disdain toward those who had not received as fair of a shake from society's tree. But the real reason these scholars scorn Cleveland is because he was not a wealth redistributionist progressive.

Many historians use a variety of unconstructive words to describe the man and his public career: lucky, stubborn, stolid, negative, inflexible, uncompromising, and unimaginative. But they save their best venom for his attitude in regard to the lower classes – farmers, artisans, laborers, pensioners, small shop owners, and minorities. One of his fiercest critics, Vincent DeSantis of Notre Dame, wrote that Cleveland's policies "appealed to the conservative businessmen" and "provided little consolation to the masses of the people. Cleveland fought the idea of the social service state." He "was an extreme conservative, and the people's quest for social justice" did not advance under Cleveland's administrations. He had "little understanding of the broader and more positive role that government could play."[17]

DeSantis has perfectly captured the real problem modern-day historians have with Grover Cleveland – he did not believe in advancing social justice or using government as a positive force in the lives of the common man to provide social services. He simply believed in the principles of the Declaration of Independence and the Constitution as crafted by the Founders. But for progressive historians, any president who believes in original intent and does not consider government a positive force is an anachronism worthy of the title "mediocre," if not outright "failure."

The Constitution, earlier Americans correctly understood, does not contain any language that allows the government to spend money for public assistance, not even the general welfare clause authorizes such acts. James Madison, the Father of the Constitution, explained on numerous occasions that the general welfare clause, so often cited by advocates of "energetic government," was not a grant of power. "If Congress can do whatever in their *discretion* can be *done by money*, and will promote the *general welfare*, the government is no longer a limited one possessing enumerated powers but an indefinite one subject to particular expressions," he wrote in 1792.[18]

When Cleveland returned to the presidency in 1893, he spoke out harshly against paternalism in his second inaugural address. He wanted to stamp out what he feared would soon become an entrenched dependence on government handouts, particularly as the Panic of 1893 had begun the previous month. "The lessons of paternalism ought to be unlearned, and the better lesson taught that while the people should patriotically and cheerfully support their government its functions do not include the support of the people," he told his fellow citizens. "Every thoughtful American must realize the importance of checking at its beginning any tendency in public or private station to regard frugality and economy as virtues we may safely outgrow. The toleration of this idea results in the waste of the people's money by their chosen servants and encourages prodigality and extravagance in the home life of our countrymen."[19]

Cleveland believed, as did all Jeffersonians, that the Constitution did not allow the federal government to spend money on public charity, and if Washington started down the road of paternalism, where would it end? And because of Cleveland's presidency, those paternalistic lessons were "unlearned" and early Jeffersonian principles held true, at least for the issue of public charity, for more than thirty years after Cleveland left the White House for the final time in 1897.

TAKING ON THE WEALTHY

Where historians and other scholars make a great mistake is in assuming that paternalism is a one-way enterprise. In Cleveland's day, the very wealthy in America donated to both parties, but it was Republicans who gained the most and had Wall Street's ear, for which the rich gained plenty of protection and influence from the GOP-administered government. While disapproving of help for the lower class, Cleveland also aggressively combated paternalism toward the wealthy. He had no problem with wealth, believing as he did in a strong work ethic, but felt that one should become rich the old-fashioned way – with innovative ideas and by the sweat of one's brow. Gaining wealth with the aid and influence of Washington, those that Professor Burton Folsom refers to as "political entrepreneurs," was not the American way, nor was it "fair." So, therefore, Cleveland cannot be regarded as a businessman's chief executive. A simple analysis of major accomplishments during Cleveland's tenure as governor of New York and president of the United States would easily prove that he approved laws for the benefit of the common man, which went against the business interests, far more than he did for the commercial and moneyed elite.[20]

As governor, he signed a law to regulate the cigar-making industry, a legislative proposal by Assemblyman Theodore Roosevelt. Despite disagreements on other concerns, Cleveland worked closely with Roosevelt on a number of important reform issues. Sitting on a three-member state assembly committee, the future trustbuster and regulator took aim at the horrid conditions of the cigar industry in New York City, all at the behest of the cigar-makers' union, headed by Samuel Gompers. Much of the industry's work was done in private, one-room homes rather than in a factory setting, with most of the workers being comprised of poor immigrants and their children. Conditions within these establishments were unsanitary and unhealthy, to put it mildly. Seeing the conditions firsthand, Roosevelt supported a bill to place regulations on the industry. Before it passed, the young TR strolled down to Governor Cleveland's office and, "acting as a spokesman for the battered undersized foreigners," hoped to persuade a "reluctant" Cleveland to sign it, even though "it was contrary to the principles of political economy of the laissez faire kind," the young assemblyman noted. The governor signed the bill, for he always did what he could legally and constitutionally for the most pitiful among us.[21]

On a number of occasions, Governor Cleveland pointed to the "injustice and discrimination" in New York's tax laws, which should receive the utmost "care and attention," he wrote to the legislature. He sought "to preserve the honor of the state in its dealings with the citizen, to prevent the rich, by shirking taxation, from adding to the burdens of the poor, and to relieve the landholder from unjust discrimination." Historians who routinely attack Cleveland as an ardent supporter of the business and financial interests over those of farmers and the poor overlook this important goal he had for a fair tax system. He believed government should be on the side of everyone, not to actively aid any individual group, but, rather, by staying out of the way, providing equal and exact justice to all. Taxes could be kept low for everyone if the legislature could "furnish the people a good government at the least possible cost."[22]

As a "most valuable protection to the people," Governor Cleveland also sought laws that would require large corporations to report their financial conditions to a state agency, much as railroad corporations had to report to the state Railroad Commission each year. Cleveland scolded the corrupt practices of big business, including the practice of lobbying.

> While the stockholders are the owners of the corporate property, notoriously they are oftentimes completely in the power of the directors and managers, who acquire a majority of the stock and by this means perpetuate their control, using the corporate property and franchise for their benefit and profit, regardless of the interests and rights of the minority of stockholders. Immense salaries are paid to officers; transactions are consummated by which the directors make money, while the rank and file among the stockholders lose it; the honest investor waits for dividends and the directors grow rich. It is suspected, too, that large sums are spent under various disguises in efforts to influence legislation.[23]

Again, this shows Cleveland was not in the back pocket of the nation's largest businesses but sought to make sure they acted with honesty and integrity, though the legislature did not act on this recommendation.

As president, he took on some of the most entrenched special interests in Washington. The government under the administration of Republicans had been very beneficent toward the railroads, the largest industry in America during the late nineteenth century. A key part of the GOP economic program was corporate subsidies, which, in truth, was nothing more than "crony capitalism." In building the transcontinental railroads, the government lavished those corporations with handouts in the form of massive loans and enormous land grants, with most of the railroad loans remaining unpaid because most of the rail companies went bankrupt. Though some of the money was repaid, in all railroad corporations made off with more than $350 million in government funds and 150 million acres of land over a period of thirty years. These programs of "bounties and subsidies," Cleveland said in his second inaugural address in 1893, "burden the labor and thrift of a portion of our citizens to aid ill-advised or languishing enterprises in which they have no concern."[24]

There would be no such enterprises in the Cleveland administration. He struck back against the railroads and seized 80 million acres of land for the public, mainly because the railroads did not live up to their end of the bargain. The few railroad tycoons who had backed Cleveland for president, like James J. Hill, thought they might receive favors in return for their support but soon found out that his support would garner him no special treatment. When Hill desired a government right-of-way to take his Great Northern railroad through an Indian reservation and sent a telegram asking the president for permission, Cleveland rejected his request. The venture would only proceed after the government negotiated with the Indians and made sure they were not the victims of fraud, so often the case throughout American history.[25]

Cleveland also signed legislation creating the Interstate Commerce Commission, which began regulating railroads and preventing them from continuing to employ what many considered discriminatory practices. Though the Interstate Commerce Commission might have been viewed as necessary to many in Washington at the time, it represented a potential threat of government encroachment into the free market, particularly under a more progressive administration. In the words of Professor Thomas DiLorenzo, the commission "soon created a bureaucratic monstrosity that attempted to micromanage all aspects of the railroad business, hampering its efficiency even further."[26]

To Independent Institute scholar Ivan Eland, the law set "a precedent for federal regulation of private economic behavior, which would expand dramatically over the next century. Cleveland thus provided the underpinning for the progressive movement, which would, in the name of progress, advocate further usurpation of individual economic and political rights – to the detriment of those it was trying to help." Though Eland's assessment may be a bit harsh, the creation of the Interstate Commerce Commission was not Cleveland's finest Jeffersonian moment and did cause major harm to laissez faire capitalism for future generations.[27]

Cleveland, though, never intended the ICC to be a monstrous federal agency. To his private secretary, George F. Parker, he confided that, after "a careful study of the question, and in spite of reservations, I signed the bill."

In what would later come to be called "presidential signing statements," he desired, upon approving the measure, to "file a memorandum setting forth my doubts on constitutional points, and explaining my conception of its limitations." Deciding against that course of action, he determined that it was better to "assume responsibility and then to see that the new system started under the most favorable auspices" and made sure that its commissioners, as well as the rules governing it "were instituted on safe and conservative lines." The original commission "did not clash with the powers of the states; it was not partisan, either in organization or direction; and did not meddle or assert authority not comprehended in its enactment or inconsistent with the theory and workings of our institutions. It did not check enterprise or initiative, nor was it used by one interest against another." Sadly, it did not long remain that way, as progressive administrations would later expand its use.[28]

As for the great continental railroad system, it was a colossal economic failure. During the late nineteenth century, five lines were constructed to connect the east coast to the west. The first four operated under the government's paternalistic system, receiving the outrageous amounts of cash and land. The results were inefficiency, cost overruns, corruption, and insolvency. All four lines went bankrupt, some more than once. The fifth, constructed by Cleveland supporter James J. Hill, used private sources to buy land and construct the entire line from Minneapolis to Seattle. It took a bit longer, but the company remained efficient, prosperous, and free of corruption, never once going broke, not even during the Panic of 1893, which took down several competitors. Government paternalism toward business has a failed track record, as history has shown, leading to corruption and inefficiency, something Cleveland and earlier Americans knew and understood well.[29]

Though the railroads had a great relationship with Washington, that subsidized program paled in comparison to another. The largest single form of government paternalism to any social class during the late nineteenth century was the high protective tariff, an early form of corporate welfare aimed at aiding those at the very top of society's ladder, notably the major industrialists. The tariff was the heart of the Republican Party's platform. End it and the party was as good as dead. So, the GOP planted its flag on the hill of high protection and would not budge from that position.

From the enactment of the Morrill Tariff in 1861, which Lincoln hiked numerous times, until 1885, Republicans controlled the government and with it tariff rates, keeping them at a very high level, near fifty percent. No Democrat occupied the White House until Cleveland, so low tariff proponents had no chance to cut taxes during their twenty-five-year period in the political wilderness. In addition to the high tariffs, Republicans expanded federal excise taxes and inflated the currency with fiat money to fund their spending schemes, like the subsidies to railroads and generous pensions to military veterans. The steady stream of revenue led to the accumulation of large surpluses, excess money the Republican Congress was all too eager to spend.

Once in office, Cleveland took on the Republican sacred cow head-on. Seeing there was no need to continue piling up huge surpluses, aside from providing Congress with ample reason to splurge, he advocated a lower tariff rate, sufficient to gain only enough revenue to fund the essentials of the federal government, applying such taxes, including excises, to luxury items while removing them from raw materials and goods deemed essential for day-to-day living, which would benefit domestic industry and the working classes. Furthermore, in the late nineteenth century, American industry was "no longer infantile," the president believed. It stood on its own two feet and needed no further protection. American products dominated the domestic market, as well as that of most foreign nations. No other country, not even the British, threatened American manufacturing supremacy. So protective tariffs, in this case, seemed to be political payoffs to mercantilist fat cats who bankrolled the GOP.[30]

In 1886, a tariff reform bill authored by Democratic Congressman William R. Morrison met defeat in the House by a vote of 157 to 140. But despite the setback, Cleveland wanted to focus intensely on his economic program and began gearing up for a major fight. In June 1887, he wrote to Tammany Hall on his tariff position. "Our government belongs to the people. They have decreed its purposes, and it is their clear right to demand that its cost shall be limited by frugality and that its burden of expenses shall be limited by its actual needs." The surplus, continually piling up in the treasury, is nothing more than "extortion on the part of the government." It was over-taxation, pure and simple. His plan would return money to the taxpayers and help everyone equally, even those at the bottom of society's rungs. Yet the opponents of tariff reform "attempt to disturb our workingmen with the cry that their wages and their employment are threatened," but they "advocate the system [that] benefits certain classes of our citizens at the expense of every householder in the land—a system [that] breeds discontentment because it permits the duplication of wealth without corresponding additional recompense to labor." A high tariff "enhances the cost of living beyond the laborers' hard-earned wages." Politicians then attempt "to divert the attention of the people from the evils of such a scheme of taxation by branding those who seek to correct these evils as free traders and enemies of our workingmen and our industrial enterprises. That is so far from the truth that there can be no chance for such deception to succeed."[31]

It was in December of that year when Cleveland's seriousness shone bright as he took the unprecedented step of sending Congress his annual message on the subject of the tariff. Gilded Age historian H. Wayne Morgan argues that Cleveland did this only because he needed a winning issue in order to gain a second term in the White House, as tariff reform "would cover the party's weaknesses" in the 1888 presidential election. Cleveland scholar Richard E. Welch Jr., author of *The Presidencies of Grover Cleveland*, concurs with Morgan and contends that by the time of the 1887 message, Cleveland had already decided to seek reelection and sought "to distract the attention of the Democratic party from the divisive issue of free silver."[32]

But these analyses are flawed. For one thing, the silver issue was not nearly as disruptive as it would be during the 1890s. What's more, Cleveland hardly needed a signature issue and certainly had no thought of politics when he decided to be bold with his message. In fact, his aides and political friends advised him *not* to send the message for fear it would hurt his reelection chances. But Cleveland would not be moved by political expediency. He sought tariff reform for philosophical and economic reasons, crafting a message that was a brilliant tribute to Jeffersonian political economy.[33]

In the nineteenth century, federal taxes came in two types – tariffs and excise taxes, both an indirect and a more direct form. The tariff was the main source of funds, accounting for 56.1 percent of federal revenue in 1885. But Cleveland believed current tariff rates were "the vicious, inequitable, and illogical source of unnecessary taxation," he told Congress in his message, and "ought to be at once revised and amended."

And by "revised and amended," he meant downward, to ease the burden on the backs of the people who bought manufactured goods, products that rose in price with high tariffs. He also wanted excise taxes to remain on expensive items, those bought by the rich and not deemed necessary for one to depend upon, and reduced on the essentials for everyday living. "The taxation of luxuries presents no features of hardship; but the necessaries of life used and consumed by all the people, the duty upon which adds to the cost of living in every home, should be greatly cheapened." With the president squarely behind the effort with his tariff message, a second attempt, the Mills Bill, survived a House vote in the spring of 1888 but met defeat in the Senate, where all tariff reduction proposals went to die in those days.[34]

But 1888 was a presidential election year, and with Republicans vowing to return to the White House, they now had an issue to use against the popular president. Cleveland's supporters had been right in the understanding that to maximize an effort on a tariff reform bill would damage him politically. To help carry their counterargument, Republicans engaged in a very aggressive fundraising campaign, hitting up large corporations for big donations. This was necessary, since being out of power deprived Republicans of the aid of federal officeholders for campaign purposes. Their fundraising tactic, applied mainly to the manufacturing interest, was simple and unveiled. If businesses desired tariff protection, they must contribute to the GOP cause. This technique became known as "frying the fat" out of corporations and was nothing more than a political shakedown. In all, the Republican Party raised millions of dollars for its battle against Cleveland. The campaign tactic worked, as the president went down to defeat against Benjamin Harrison, though Cleveland won the most popular votes. But having lost the election, he felt no regret in having pushed an issue he'd felt strongly about.[35]

"THE BILLION-DOLLAR CONGRESS"

During Cleveland's first term in office, he had struck back against a quarter century of Republican governance. He cleaned up corruption, ended presidential luxury, slashed the bureaucracy, halted out-of-control spending by vetoing a record 414 bills, protected the massive budget surplus that Republicans were all too eager to spend, attempted to cut taxes by a significant margin only to come up short in the US Senate, and reduced the national debt by twenty percent. After four years of Jeffersonian governance by Grover Cleveland, progressive Republicans were back in charge of the White House and both houses of Congress after their narrow victory in 1888.

When Benjamin Harrison entered office in March 1889, with a Congress controlled by the GOP, Republicans wasted little time in getting its energetic government agenda back on track. The Jeffersonian interlude of Grover Cleveland only made Republicans more eager, and with full control of the federal government once again, they embarked on an ambitious, far-reaching agenda, seemingly to make up for lost time. The new House Speaker, Thomas "Czar" Reed of Maine, summed up the Republican attitude about governance. "The danger in a free country is not that power will be exercised too freely," he said, "but that it will be exercised too sparingly."[36]

During the first session of the Fifty-First Congress, which sat from 1889 to 1890, Republicans enacted several major pieces of legislation. They inflated the currency, raised taxes, massively increased spending, squandered the surplus, tried to assert federal control over local issues, and even went after some corporations with a historic new law. They even re-started "sectional warfare" by passing laws to increase the premiums paid to war bondholders and to return federal tax money paid by the Northern states during the war, issues that would only anger the South.[37]

First, to provide more inflation in the currency, pressure that also came from the West, Congress passed the Sherman Silver Purchase Act, which required the government to buy four and a half million ounces of silver per month, the total amount produced by the nation's silver mines in the western states. Under the previous silver law, the Bland-Allison Act of 1878, the government purchased just two million ounces per month. Though not all of the silver was coined and put into circulation, the Sherman Act authorized new treasury notes to purchase the bullion, greenbacks that could be redeemed for gold. The infusion of new money produced a boom period, but it also caused a slow drain on the nation's gold reserve, which, along with too much cheap money in the economy and increased spending, would lead to a severe depression in 1893.

Second, protectionist Republicans wanted an increase in tariffs, even though rates were already at all-time highs. Ohio Congressman William McKinley, chairman of the House Ways and Means Committee, authored a new tariff law that raised duties to their highest level in history. By doing so, it was hoped the McKinley Act would keep out most foreign imports, which would take away all competition for American businesses and also help alleviate the growing federal budget surplus, ongoing since 1866. With such high rates, imports would fall, thereby diminishing revenue. Western Republicans, not necessarily in favor of higher tariffs, supported the measure in exchange for eastern support for the silver act. But despite the bill's intention, the tariff's high duties effectively raised taxes on everyone by making products more expensive for consumers.

Third, in another effort to get rid of the pesky surplus, Congress passed an extravagant pension bill, the Dependent Pension Act, to provide help to Union army veterans and their dependents, essentially the same one vetoed by President Cleveland in 1887. Older, more stringent requirements were loosened tremendously so that anyone who had served at least ninety days in the Union army during the Civil War and had a disability, regardless of how the handicap occurred, could receive a pension. The new Republican Congress, now in conjunction with a Republican president, placed it on the law books to reward one of its favored constituent groups with funds from the public trough.

Under Harrison and the Republican Congress, spending on pensions rose from $80 million in 1888, Cleveland's last full year of his first term, to $160 million by 1893, when Cleveland resumed the presidency. The pension list also swelled from 489,725 recipients in 1889 to 966,012 in 1893 as the Pension Bureau added 19,000 new pensioners per *month*, whereas before just 19,000 per *year* were placed to the rolls, as everyone with army experience rushed to get on the dole.[38]

In addition to the increased spending on pensions, Congress appropriated a wealth of money for other schemes, earmarking funds for additional naval vessels and various internal improvements projects, such as river and harbor development, the main pork barrel project of the day. With all the spending, Democrats quickly dubbed it the "Billion-Dollar Congress," the first Congress in American history to spend a billion dollars. Czar Reed, smug and arrogant, responded to Democratic criticism of the splurge by noting, "It's a billion-dollar country!"[39]

Under this more energetic governance, the nation saw its hard-earned surplus, accumulating in the treasury at a rate of $100 million per year, vanish with scarcely a return. While in office, Cleveland had watched over it like a protective mother and tried on many occasions to return it to the people, but Republicans squandered it with little regard for its rightful owners. In 1888, Cleveland's final year in office, the surplus amounted to $111 million; after Harrison's administration it had dwindled to just $2 million. One political cartoon of the day depicted President Harrison pouring Cleveland's surplus into a large hole in the ground.[40]

Fourth, the Republican Congress also attempted to assert federal control over traditionally local issues. One bill, authored by Republican Senator Henry W. Blair of New Hampshire, provided $15 million in federal aid to education, a proposal he had submitted in every Congress since 1881. President Harrison supported the measure, but it was defeated in the Senate by a narrow vote of 42 to 36.[41]

Another bill authored by Congressman Henry Cabot Lodge of Massachusetts would have given the federal courts jurisdiction over state and local elections as well as registration efforts, presumably to aid disenfranchised blacks in the South. But Democrats feared the measure would enhance the GOP's hold on power through fraud. Southerners, reminded of the hated days of Reconstruction, were outraged, calling the act the "Force Bill." It passed the House by a close party-line vote but later died in the Senate. Cleveland called the proposal to control elections "a dark blow at the freedom of the ballot."[42]

And fifth, Republicans, succumbing to pressure from its western base, authorized the Sherman Antitrust Act, a strong measure that gave the federal government more control over big business. Authored by Senator John Sherman of Ohio, brother of the famous general, the bill stated: "Every contract, combination in the form of trust or otherwise, or conspiracy, in restraint of trade or commerce among the several States, or with foreign nations, is hereby declared to be illegal." Such vague language in the new law allowed future administrations, namely that of Theodore Roosevelt, to expand it and use it in wide-ranging ways. With this bill, the federal government could essentially seize and break up any company it deemed a monopoly. It "was one of the most important enactments ever passed by Congress," wrote Republican Senator Shelby Cullom of Illinois, but "if it were strictly and literally enforced, the business of the country would come to a standstill." The federal power grab was enormous.[43]

Democrats across the country were angered at Republican efforts to accrue even more power in Washington, and Cleveland, as the only living ex-president from that party, was much sought after for advice and support on how to combat it. Hesitant to actively campaign for candidates, the former chief executive counseled his party to remain on the sidelines. There was no need to offer Democratic alternatives, he told them. Republicans had sought control of the government, and now they had it, so he recommended patience, for it wouldn't be long, Cleveland believed, before the people were alerted to GOP shenanigans.

Though Cleveland counseled restraint, the Republican legislative program, particularly the spending, greatly concerned him, because it looked as though his four years of hard work was going down the drain. But, in the end, he thought it might work out for the best. "You and others used to say that our administration of affairs would be remembered long by the American people," he wrote to William Vilas, one of his former cabinet secretaries, who became a close friend and pen pal during these intervening years. "I could not see why this should necessarily be so; but our successors have made it so, I am sure. I feel badly and sad to see the result of so much hard labor undone. And yet I sometimes think that God has ordered it all for the enlightenment and awakening of our people."[44]

On another occasion he wrote to Vilas, "In these days, the people who occupy in Washington are so fast running off the rope, which I believe is bound to get about their necks." So why interfere with a party that was in the process of committing suicide? "I have thought as I have seen the Republicans getting deeper and deeper into the mire that our policy should be to let them flounder," he wrote Congressman John Carlisle.[45]

Cleveland's political instincts proved to be right, as the massive GOP program proved too much for the American people. In the midterm elections in 1890, Republicans were trounced in one of the greatest midterm landslides, losing more than ninety seats in the House. Conservative Democrats won an astonishing 238 of 332 congressional races. When the Fifty-Second Congress opened in 1891, only eighty-six Republicans remained in the US House of Representatives. Among the vanquished: staunch progressive and future presidential candidate Robert M. LaFollette of Wisconsin; future House Speaker Joseph "Uncle Joe" Cannon of Illinois; and future president William McKinley, who was punished for his massive tax hike. One of the new Democratic arrivals was a young, thirty-six-year-old populist from Lincoln, Nebraska named William Jennings Bryan. And though they did not reclaim the Senate,

Democrats gained four seats there as well. Happily relaxing in retirement, Cleveland was overjoyed with the electoral success and wrote a close friend, "Election news and fishing rods make me quite happy in these days. Did you ever see such a landslide?" The "Billion Dollar Congress" had set the stage for the presidential election of 1892.[46]

THE RISE OF "ME TOO" DEMOCRATS

As the leading Democrat in the country, Cleveland was asked to again be a candidate for the White House, but he had no desire to return to what he often referred to as a "killing office." But two things changed his mind: he did not like what the Republicans were doing to the country and he was greatly disturbed by the movement within the Democratic Party to emulate GOP policies, a nineteenth-century version of "me too" politics. Leading Democratic presidential candidates in 1892 were moving toward the Republicans on the issues of protectionism and currency inflation with an advocacy of free coinage of silver. These policies, Cleveland believed, would hurt the people and destroy his party. That he could not and would not allow.

Soon he began giving public speeches articulating the philosophy that set Democrats apart from Republicans and made it the party that should be in power in Washington. On January 8, 1891, he gave a Jackson Day public address in Philadelphia at the Young Men's Democratic Association, a speech titled "The Principles of True Democracy," a clear enunciation of the Jeffersonian Ideal. The true principles of the Democratic Party were a creed, he told his assembled audience, a creed that had the significance of religious dogma, and were not to be violated. The Democratic Creed was not "uncertain or doubtful" but came straight from the "illustrious founder of our party," Mr. Jefferson:

> Equal and exact justice to all men; peace, commerce, and honest friendship with all nations—entangling alliance with none; the support of the State governments in all their rights; the preservation of the general government in its whole constitutional vigor; a jealous care of the right of election by the people; absolute acquiescence in the decisions of the majority; the supremacy of the civil over the military authority; economy in the public expenses; the honest payment of our debts and sacred preservation

of the public faith; the encouragement of agriculture, and commerce as its handmaid, and freedom of religion, freedom of the press, and freedom of the person.[47]

But the party had begun moving away from these timeless principles, he believed, and the federal government was now engaged in government paternalism, siding with one class of Americans over another, namely in exorbitant spending, and in crushing the rights of the states and the people. When "we see the functions of government used to enrich a favored few at the expense of many," he said, "and see also its inevitable result in the pinching privation of the poor and the profuse extravagance of the rich; and when we see in operation an unjust tariff which banishes from many humble homes the comforts of life, in order that, in the palaces of wealth, luxury may more abound, we turn to our creed and find that it enjoins "equal and exact justice to all men." He continued:

> When we see our farmers in distress, and know that they are not paying the penalty of slothfulness and mismanagement, when we see their long hours of toil so poorly requited that the money lender eats out their substance, while for everything they need to pay a tribute to the favorites of governmental care, we know that all this is far removed from the "encouragement of agriculture," which our creed commands.

> When we see the extravagance of public expenditure fast reaching the point of reckless waste, and the undeserved distribution of public money debauching its recipients, and by pernicious example threatening the destruction of the love of frugality among our people, we will remember that "economy in the public expense" is an important article in the true Democratic faith.

> When we see our political adversaries bent upon the passage of a Federal law, with the scarcely denied purpose of perpetuating partisan supremacy, which invades the States with election machinery designed to promote Federal interference with the rights of the people in the localities concerned, discrediting their honesty and fairness, and justly arousing their jealousy of centralized power, we will stubbornly resist such a dangerous and

revolutionary scheme, in obedience to our pledge for "the support of the State governments in all their rights."

With strict adherence to such principles, the party, back in power once again, and "by an intelligent study of existing conditions, should be prepared to meet all the wants of the people as they arise, and to furnish a remedy for every threatening evil." The government existed, he believed, and the people supported it "for the sake of the benefits of all," not to the chosen few, whomever they may be. The protection of the people's rights and the promotion of their welfare and happiness was the object of good government, and, he believed, only the Democratic Party, with its adherence to "time-honored principles," could obtain it.

The American people, who always stood with him, agreed. Two years after the Republicans and their "Billion-Dollar Congress" came to an end in November 1890, the Harrison administration felt the wrath of the American people. Cleveland would occupy the White House for a second time and was once again determined to keep the ideals of the American Revolution, embodied in the Party of Jefferson, alive and well in the United States.

THE CLASS CARD

Even in Cleveland's day, the opposition would resort to using class as a political weapon. United States Supreme Court Justice Stephen J. Field prophesied about the use of class warfare in a harsh concurring opinion that struck down the nation's first peacetime income tax law in 1895, a proposal enacted with wealth redistribution in mind. He saw the real danger in such a tax. "The present assault on capital is but the beginning," he wrote. "It will be but the stepping-stone to others, larger and more sweeping, till our political contests will become a war of the poor against the rich; a war constantly growing in intensity and bitterness."[48]

Before his departure from the White House after his defeat at the hands of the Republicans, Cleveland used his final State of the Union message to Congress, in December 1888, to discuss the great disparity of wealth in the country. "Upon more careful inspection we find the wealth and luxury of our cities mingled with poverty and wretchedness and unremunerative toil," he wrote. Because of government action in prior administrations, the vast "fortunes realized by our manufacturers are no longer solely the reward of sturdy industry and enlightened foresight, but ... the discriminating favor of the government and are largely built upon undue exactions from the masses of our people." As a result, the "gulf between employers and the employed is constantly widening, and classes are rapidly forming, one comprising the very rich and powerful, while in another are found the toiling poor." The wealthy existed under "trusts, combinations, and monopolies, while the citizen is struggling far in the rear or is trampled to death beneath an iron heel. Corporations, which should be the carefully restrained creatures of the law and the servants of the people, are fast becoming the people's masters." This arrangement was simply unfair to the average taxpayer and, what's more, it would produce an unstable class-based society that, "when fully realized, will surely arouse irritation and discontent." He could clearly see the potential political use of the infamous class card.[49]

Cleveland believed, as he had long advocated, that most of these problems could be corrected – not by any program on the part of the government to redistribute wealth but by a fairer system of taxation. Though he had just recently lost reelection while arguing that very cause, he continued to pound on the tariff and tax issues and the unjust inequality he found in the current system. "Instead of limiting the tribute drawn from our citizens to the necessities of its economical administration," he told Congress, "the government persists in exacting from the substance of the people millions which, unapplied and useless, lie dormant in its Treasury" in the form of a surplus. The present system "is not equality before the law."

The result of such an unjust system might result in a variety of communism, which, to Cleveland, was "a hateful thing and a menace to peace and organized government." However, it would not be the traditional form advocated in Europe but "the communism of combined wealth and capital, the outgrowth of overweening cupidity and selfishness, which insidiously undermines the justice and integrity of free institutions." This form "is not less dangerous than the communism of oppressed poverty and toil, which, exasperated by injustice and discontent, attacks with wild disorder the citadel of rule." As Cleveland biographer Alyn Brodsky has noted, "No other president before (or since) had spoken so radically on the disparity between the haves and the have-nots."[50]

But Brodsky's analysis of Cleveland's remark is not accurate, as he insinuated that President Cleveland was "prepared ... to see the imposition of stringent curbs upon wealth." No program to limit the accumulation of wealth was ever enunciated by Cleveland. He believed that the disparity of wealth, with its possible communistic outcome, resulted in those at the bottom of the socioeconomic spectrum, the very ones Grover Cleveland supposedly detested, not deriving the same benefits from the government as those at the top. The government, mainly through the tariff and burdensome taxation, aided the rich in gaining more wealth. America's farmers and other laborers, who were "struggling in the race of life with the hardest and most unremitting toil, will not fail to see, in spite of misrepresentations and misleading fallacies ... that without compensating favor they are forced by the action of the government to pay for the benefit of others such enhanced prices for the things they need that the scanty returns of their labor fail to furnish their support or leave no margin for accumulation." Only an equitable tax system and an end to government paternalism would fix the situation, thereby growing the nation's wealth for all.[51]

Cleveland's economic policy sought to return to "the principles of true Democracy because they are founded in patriotism and upon justice and fairness toward all interests," he wrote in a letter to Mississippi Congressman Thomas C. Catchings. He sought a system that favored no one and a government that treated everyone fairly and equally. This alone would ensure an equitable system, the very structure crafted by the Founding Fathers. That was Grover Cleveland's single aim as president.

MAN OF THE PEOPLE

Grover Cleveland rose to the presidency from modest means, using the virtues of hard work and determination, not privileges and handouts. He possessed very little formal education, receiving most of his instruction from his father in a home-school setting. And because of his circumstances, a college education proved beyond his reach. But he labored to make something of himself and believed everyone could do likewise. He believed that the government should take no side, not for big business or small business, nor for the farmer or the laborer. The government should treat everyone equally. That is precisely why he hated the protective tariff system, because it favored the business class over the working class.

For Cleveland, the government existed for a certain purpose as outlined in the Constitution and nothing more. The government should see all citizens the same way, regardless of class or race or any other distinction. He believed in equality before the law. The government was there to see that the economy ran smoothly, that commerce flowed freely, that the money supply was stable, that foreign affairs were appropriately handled, and, above all others, that individual liberty was always protected. It did not exist to enrich one class of citizens at the expense of another. If the government handled its constitutional duties, the people could take care of their own lives.

And the plain folks throughout the country praised him for his principled stand as a "man of the people." A *New York Times* reporter visited Kentucky in the spring of 1891, at a time when it was heavily rumored that Cleveland might seek a second presidential term, and described the former president's support as very strong, noting that "it would take a search warrant to discover a Democrat opposed to the re-nomination of Cleveland." Speaking with an old Kentucky farmer, who was a well-read and educated man, the reporter learned just how strongly the common man in the Bluegrass State held him. "Cleveland is the man; he is the third link of the Democratic chain: Jefferson, Jackson, Cleveland," the farmer said. The plain people, he continued, will not "permit that New York crowd of traders to dictate to us." The people wanted one of their own as their president, not a candidate of Wall Street. They trusted Cleveland to look out for their interests.[52]

John Goode of Virginia, who served in the US House from 1875 to 1881 and then later as Cleveland's solicitor general, also discovered the working-class affinity for Cleveland firsthand. Questioning an "old Democrat from the county of Grayson" at the Virginia state Democratic convention, Goode inquired as to which Democrat the plain people, those "who live in log cabins on the mountainside" in the Old Dominion, supported for president. "Why, they are all for Cleveland," the old gentleman responded. "Every time any of the speakers made reference to Mr. Cleveland, the applause of the people was so great that it seemed to me they would take the roof off the courthouse," he continued. Intrigued, Goode then asked why such enthusiastic support for Cleveland. The old Democrat promptly listed three reasons. "In the first place, they say he is honest; in the second place, they say he is the poor man's friend; and in the third place, they say he is the boss dog in the tan yard," meaning he stood up to the special interests in Washington. So, despite the opinions of academic historians, the plain folk were with Cleveland and he was always with them.[53]

Endnotes

1   Thomas Jefferson to Thomas Cooper, November 29, 1802, in *Writings*, X, 342.

2   *Boston Herald*, June 8, 1880.

3   Rutherford B. Hayes, Diary Entry, January 24, 1886, in Charles Richard Williams, ed., *The Diary and Letters of Rutherford B. Hayes, Nineteenth President of the United States* (Columbus, Ohio: Ohio State Archeological and Historical Society, 1922), IV, 261-2.

4   Donald L. McMurray, *Coxey's Army: A Study of the Industrial Army Movement of 1894* (Boston: Brown, Little & Company, 1929), 22, 25-6.

5   Cleveland to Hon. William L. Wilson, and others, Committee, etc., Letter of Acceptance, September 26, 1892, *Official Proceedings of the National Democratic Convention*, edited by Edward B. Dickinson (Chicago: Cameron, Amberg & Co., 1892), 234-40.

6   Cleveland, "Veto of Texas Seed Bill," February 16, 1887, Richardson, ed., *Messages and Papers*, XI, 5142-3.

7   *Houston Daily Post*, February 18, 1887; *Dallas Morning News*, February 17, 1887.

8   Marvin Olasky, *The American Leadership Tradition: Moral Vision from Washington to Clinton* (New York: The Free Press, 1999), 160.

9   Beatty, 195.

10   *Ibid.*

11   William H. Glasson, *Federal Military Pensions in the United States* (New York: Oxford University Press, 1918), 277; Philip Leigh, *Southern Reconstruction* (Yardley, Pennsylvania: Westholme Publishing, 2017), xvii.

12   Glasson, 277; Keller, 311.

13   Leigh, xvii; Cleveland, Veto of a Pension Bill for William Bishop, June 23, 1886, Richardson, ed., *Messages and Papers*, XI, 5028.

14   Cleveland, Veto of a Pension Bill for Cudbert Stone, February 4, 1887, *Ibid.*, 5131-2; Cleveland, Veto of a Pension Bill for John W. Farris, June 21, 1886, *Ibid.*, 5020-1; Cleveland, Veto of a Pension Bill for William H. Hester, May 19, 1888,

Ibid., 5252; Cleveland, Veto of a Pension Bill for Rebecca Eldridge, May 28, 1886, Richardson, ed., Messages and Papers, XI, 5009-10.

15   Donald L. McMurry, "The Political Significance of the Pension Question," *Mississippi Valley Historical Review* (June 1922), 21, 23; Glasson, 331; *New York Times*, February 8, 1887.

16   Cleveland, Veto of the Dependent Pension Bill, February 11, 1887, Richardson, ed., *Messages and Papers*, XI, 5134-5142; Nevins, *Cleveland*, 330-331.

17   Vincent P. De Santis, "Grover Cleveland," in Borden, ed., *America's Eleven Greatest Presidents*, 162-4.

18   James Madison to Edmund Pendleton, January 21, 1792, *Papers of James Madison: Congressional Series*, edited by Robert A. Rutland et al, (Charlottesville: University Press of Virginia, 1983), Volume 14, 195-6. Emphasis in the original.

19   Cleveland, Second Inaugural Address, March 4, 1893, Richardson, ed., *Messages and Papers*, XII, 5821-25.

20   Burton Folsom, *The Myth of the Robber Barons* (Herndon, VA, 1991), 132.

21   Theodore Roosevelt, *Autobiography*, edited by Louis Auchincloss (New York: Library of America edition, 2004), 333-334.

22   Cleveland, Second Message to the New York Legislature, *Public Papers of Grover Cleveland, Governor, 1883*-1884, 2 vols. (Albany: Argus Company, Printers, 1883), II, 3-59.

23   *Ibid.*

24   Carter Goodrich, *Government Promotion of Canals and Railroads, 1800-1900* (Westport, Connecticut: Greenwood Press, 1974), 271; Cleveland, Second Inaugural Address, March 4, 1893, Richardson, ed., *Messages and Papers*, XII, 5821-25.

25   Burton W. Folsom, Jr., *The Myth of the Robber Barons: A New Look at the Rise of Big Business in America* (Herndon, VA: Young America's Foundation, 1996), 18; Goodrich, 271.

26   Thomas J. DiLorenzo, *How Capitalism Saved America: The Untold History of Our Country, From the Pilgrims to the Present* (New York: Crown Forum, 2004),120.

27   Eland, 170.

28   Parker, *Recollections*, 296-8.

29   For more on the failure of the transcontinental lines, see Burton W. Folsom, *The Myth of the Robber Barons*, 17-39; and Thomas J. DiLorenzo, *How Capitalism Saved America*, 116-21.

30   Cleveland to Charles L. Seeger, May 30, 1890, Nevins, *Letters*, 224-5.

31   Cleveland to the Tammany Society, June 29, 1887, in Everett P. Wheeler, *Sixty Years of American Life: Taylor To Roosevelt, 1850 to 1910* (New York: E. P. Dutton & Company, 1917), 132-3.

32   H. Wayne Morgan, *Hayes to McKinley*, 271; Richard E. Welch Jr., *The Presidencies of Grover Cleveland* (Lawrence: University Press of Kansas, 1988), 85.

33   Cleveland, Third Annual Message to Congress, December 1887.

34   Alfred E. Eckes, *Opening America's Market: US Foreign Trade Policy Since 1776* (Chapel Hill: University of North Carolina Press, 1995), 49. According to data in *Historical Statistics of the United States*, government revenue in 1885 amounted to $323 million, of which $181 million came via customs duties. See Volume V, 83.

35   Gould, *Grand Old Party*, 105; Charles Calhoun, *Minority Victory: Gilded Age Politics and the Front Porch Campaign of 1888* (Lawrence, Kansas: University Press of Kansas, 2008), 126, 128.

36   Gould, *Grand Old Party*, 106.

37   Steven R. Weisman, *The Great Tax Wars: Lincoln to Wilson—The Fierce Battles over Money and Power that Transformed the Nation* (New York: Simon & Schuster, 2002), 115.

38   DiLorenzo, "The Last Good Democrat"; Schweikart and Allen, *Patriot's History*, 449; Susan Carter, et al., eds., *Historical Statistics of the United States* (New York: Cambridge University Press, 2006), V, 92.

39   Gould, *Grand Old Party*, 109.

40   Susan B. Carter, et al., eds., *Historical Statistics of the United States*, 5 volumes. (Cambridge: Cambridge University Press, 2006), V, 80-1.

41   Gould, *Grand Old Party*, 108.

42   Homer E. Socolafsky and Allan B. Spetter, *The Presidency of Benjamin Harrison* (Lawrence, Kansas: University Press of Kansas, 1987), 65-8.

43 Sherman Antitrust Act, "Our Documents, http://www.ourdocuments.gov/doc.php?doc=51; Cullom, 254.

44 Cleveland to Vilas, September 15, 1889, Nevins, *Letters*, 210–11.

45 Cleveland to Vilas, September 15, 1889, Cleveland to Representative John G. Carlisle, April 7, 1890, Nevins, *Letters*, 210–11 and 221–2.

46 Gould, *Grand Old Party*, 110; Cleveland to L. Clarke Davis, November 5, 1890, Nevins, *Letters*, 233. The House in the Fifty-First Congress consisted of 179 Republicans and 152 Democrats; the Fifty-Second would seat 238 Democrats, 86 Republicans, and 8 Populists.

47 Grover Cleveland, Speech, "The Principles of True Democracy," Parker, ed., *Writings and Speeches*, 263–71.

48 Keller, 308.

49 Cleveland, Fourth Annual Message (First Term), Richardson, ed., *Messages and Papers*, XI, 5358-5385.

50 Brodsky, 241.

51 *Ibid.*; Cleveland, Fourth Annual Message (First Term), Richardson, ed., *Messages and Papers*, XI, 5358-5385.

52 *New York Times*, April 13, 1891.

53 John Goode, *Recollections of a Lifetime* (New York: The Neale Publishing Company, 1906), 173-4.

Chapter 4

How Cleveland Used Conservatism to End an Economic Panic

"Specie is the most perfect medium because it will preserve its own level; because, having intrinsic and universal value, it can never die in our hands."

—Thomas Jefferson to John W. Epps,
November 6, 1813

"I want a currency that is stable and safe in the hands of our people. I will not knowingly be implicated in a condition that will make me in the least degree answerable to any laborer or farmer in the United States for a shrinkage in the purchasing power of the dollar he has received for a full dollar's worth of work or for a good dollar's worth of the product of his toil."

—Cleveland to Governor W. J. Northern,
September 25, 1893

Throughout the nineteenth and early twentieth centuries, economic depressions, called "panics" in those days, occurred in approximate twenty-year intervals—1819, 1837, 1857, 1873, 1893, 1907, and 1929. Prior to the market crash in October 1929, the federal government did not intervene in economic downturns. Politicians keep their "hands off," a policy known as "laissez faire," thereby allowing the market to remain free and correct itself. This very conservative approach kept the earliest depressions from lasting nearly as long as the Great Depression of the

1930s, when the government engaged in a massive intervention to "save capitalism." In most cases the panics lasted less than a presidential term and never more than multiple administrations.

THE PANIC OF 1893

During his second term, President Cleveland faced a very severe economic depression, a speculative boom and subsequent bust caused by an imbalance in the nation's credit and currency. Upon Cleveland's inauguration on March 4, 1893, the realization that things were not right in the economy soon came to fruition as major financial houses and railroads began to fail. And although many historians argue otherwise, President Cleveland ended the Panic of 1893 quickly, and he did so, not with a massive infusion of government, but with free-market principles.

The currency issue, almost always the culprit in depressions, occupied much of President Cleveland's time in the White House during both of his administrations. The monetary system in the late nineteenth century was vastly different from our present structure. Before the days of the Federal Reserve, Congress made decisions about inflating the currency. Every few years they passed laws to put more currency into circulation, decided which type would be used, and when it needed to be restricted. Whereas the United States currently circulates Federal Reserve Notes, backed by nothing but the confidence of the people, in Cleveland's day the United States operated under a system whereby both gold and silver coins, known as "specie," circulated, as well as "Greenbacks," or paper dollars, which had the backing of gold since the 1870s. Throughout his public career, Cleveland consistently advocated a sound monetary policy, staunchly supporting the gold standard, and fought any attempt to over-inflate the currency with silver or paper money.

But first a little background on the nation's monetary policy and the conditions that caused the panic. American currency had been tied to gold until the rise of Abraham Lincoln to the presidency in 1861. Though historically known as the "gatekeepers of the gold standard," the Republican Party had inflationary ideas that essentially ended gold's supremacy. In 1862, to help finance the war against the South, as well as their other spending schemes, Republicans, with the urging of Treasury Secretary Salmon P. Chase, passed the Legal Tender Act, an inflationary plan that allowed for the creation and circulation of a national paper currency, known as "Greenbacks," which did not have the backing of gold, though the Constitution specifically gives Congress the authority to "coin money," not to print it. In total, Congress issued more than $450 million in paper dollars during the four-year conflict, producing enough inflation to double the cost of living in the North. The United States had not seen that level of inflation since the days of the American Revolution with the old, worthless Continental dollar.[1]

In 1869, the United States Supreme Court ruled the Legal Tender Act unconstitutional in the case of *Hepburn v. Griswold*, preventing the issuance of paper dollars. The Chief Justice in that case, who sided with the majority, was none other than former Treasury Secretary Salmon P. Chase. The decision angered inflationist Republicans in Congress and they quickly devised a scheme to reverse the Court's ruling. Just a few years before the ruling, in a move to prevent the hated Andrew Johnson from naming any justices to the Court, Congress, using its constitutional authority, had taken away two of the Court's seats when they became vacant, for no other reason than to keep the Southern-born president from naming any new justices. But with Republican Ulysses S. Grant in the White House at the time of the *Hepburn* ruling, Congress added the two seats back to the Court, thereby raising the number of seats to its present total of nine. President Grant then nominated two new Stalwart Republican justices in 1870 in an effort to "pack it," and the court reversed itself that same year, in *Knox v. Lee*, allowing Congress the authority to issue paper currency.[2]

Sound money Republicans, however, returned the nation to the gold standard within a decade. In 1873, Congress, in an overwhelming vote by both houses, enacted the Coinage Act, which demonetized silver. Silverites, mostly Southern Democrats and Western Republicans, who represented poor farmers in need of inflationary measures, were livid and denounced the new law as the "Crime of '73." In 1875, Congress passed the Specie Resumption Act, which would redeem greenbacks with gold beginning January 1, 1879, thereby putting the United States back on a true gold standard.[3]

Democrats, more conservative than their GOP counterparts, were traditionally stronger supporters of a gold-backed, sound money policy than were the more liberal Republicans. As Yale Professor Ray B. Westerfield has written, "Every silver act that was passed – the Bland-

Allison Act of 1878 and the Sherman Compulsory Silver Purchase Act of 1890 – was passed during and by Republican administrations." Gold Democrats reigned supreme in their party until the emergence of the "silver-tongued orator" William Jennings Bryan in 1896, when the party endorsed the free coinage of silver. But like Republicans, Democratic inflationary elements began emerging much earlier, during the war years of the mid-1860s. Ohio Congressman George Pendleton, who received the party's vice-presidential nomination in 1864, backed a plan called the "Ohio Idea," a scheme to pay government bonds in greenbacks, not gold. The plan failed, but Pendleton, campaigning on inflation, attempted to gain the Democratic presidential nomination in 1868, but lost to Governor Horatio Seymour, a sound moneyman from New York. At that time, the party of Jefferson and Jackson was not ready to give up its traditional support of sound currency. But with harder economic times in the South and West, brought on by deflation, Democrats, strongest in the South but also heavily represented out on the western frontier, eventually became the main backers of the inflationary silver policy.[4]

The situation worsened with the Panic of 1873. Since 1861, the federal government, along with the states and localities, began pumping hundreds of millions of dollars into railroad construction, thereby creating an artificial bubble, which, like all government-inflated scams, finally burst in the fall of 1873. With Congress demonetizing silver just months before the panic hit, Democratic inflationists had a mighty weapon with which to attack the ruling Republicans, and they used it. In 1878, responding to rising public pressure and the discovery of new silver mines out West, Congress passed the Bland-Allison Act to begin the limited purchase and coinage of silver, in the hopes of alleviating the stresses of deflation.[5]

It was this new element of silver in the economy that Cleveland and other Jeffersonians knew would eventually cause trouble. When he first entered office in 1885, the US Treasury continued to purchase and coin silver, under Bland-Allison, at a congressionally mandated ratio of 16-to-1, meaning sixteen ounces of silver equaled one ounce of gold at the US Mint. But the real ratio, at the bullion market, reached as high as 20-to-1. So, this meant that silver was overvalued at the mint, requiring more silver to buy gold on the market. This being the case, sixteen ounces of silver could be taken to the mint to exchange for gold, flooding the treasury with silver. The one ounce of gold purchased at the mint could then be taken to the bullion market and exchanged for twenty ounces of silver, a profit of twenty-five percent on each transaction. Foreigners also contributed to this problem, bringing silver into the country to exchange for American gold. Gold, then, flowed out of the treasury while cheap silver flooded in. Cleveland had warned of this day throughout his first term, prophesying that silver could one day replace government gold in the treasury if the silver purchases were not stopped, but Congress paid little heed to his words.

As part of their big government scheme, the "Billion-Dollar Congress" in 1890 inflated the currency yet again with passage of the Sherman Silver Purchase Act, a law that mandated the government purchase all the nation's silver bullion and pay for it with new paper currency to the tune of $50 million per year. The government also continued to coin silver for circulation. This only worsened the inflation as ratios eventually reached 32-to-1.

Scholars in a wide variety of academic fields have always been in disagreement over what caused the downturn of the 1890s but generally agree that it resulted not from one source, like the level of money, but from a number of factors, such as an overexpansion of industry, over-investment in railroads, declining farm prices, and falling incomes. "The depression had more fundamental causes than the volume of the nation's currency," writes Richard E. Welch Jr. "It was primarily the product of problems in international markets of trade and finance, the overexpansion of the agricultural and transportation sectors of the US economy, and a banking system that failed to provide a necessary measure of central authority and regional cooperation." But most of these listed reasons cannot be considered the ultimate root of the problem, only symptoms of the depression.[6]

The source was something else entirely, namely too much cheap currency in circulation. "Uneasiness about the shift from gold to silver and the continuing free-silver agitation caused foreigners to lose further confidence in the US gold standard and to cause a drop in capital imports and severe gold outflows from the country," noted economist Murray Rothbard in his book *A History of Money and Banking in the United States*. "This loss of confidence exerted contractionist pressure on the American economy and reduced potential economic growth during the early 1890s." It was this policy of currency expansion that led to speculation, providing for the overexpansion of industry and the over-investment in railroads, mainly from government intervention, thereby causing an eventual drop in farm prices and declining incomes when the economy began to contract.[7]

Many astute businessmen at the time were well aware that the inflationary scheme would cause major problems in the economy. Wealthy financier Henry Villard knew from the start that the Sherman silver law "would before long plunge the whole country into general disaster." He advised friends as early as 1891 to "abstain from all long engagements, and to keep their investments in the United States in as liquid a form as possible." The "blackest clouds were gathering fast and would burst before long and sweep like a devastating tornado over the whole land," he said. He advised all he spoke with "to put their houses in order, and especially to keep out of debt and new ventures, and prepare for the worst."[8]

Yet the average American, as well as many politicians, saw only prosperity as 1893 dawned. All the new cash injected into the economy initially acted as an impetus for rapid growth. Unemployment, which stood at 5.4 percent in 1891, dropped nearly 2.5 points to 3.0 in 1892, a remarkably low figure. The nation's exports rose by $150 million in the same year, a full percent of GNP. And despite the increased spending by the Harrison administration, the national debt stood at just $961.432 million in 1893, its post–Civil War low point. By contrast, in 1885, Cleveland's first year as president, it had been more than $1.5 billion, which he cut to $1.2 billion. The nation seemed to be doing well, at least on the surface.[9]

And President Harrison made note of the excellent economic growth in his final message to Congress on December 6, 1892, a month after his loss to Cleveland. A "high degree of prosperity and so general a diffusion of the comforts of life were never before enjoyed by our people," he wrote. "There never has been a time in our history when work was so abundant or when wages were as high." Even agriculture, which always struggled in the late nineteenth century, gained "a fair participation in the general prosperity." But the affluence, noted reformer Carl Schurz, "produced the usual effect of inciting recklessness in borrowing and lending, and of stimulating the spirit of venturesome enterprise." Harrison failed to see the clear warning signs that the nation's financial success would be short-lived, as a speculative bubble had formed held up by a flurry of treasury notes and silver, all redeemable in gold.[10]

Grover Cleveland, both a former president and a president-elect, was just a few weeks shy of moving back into the White House for the second time, on March 4, 1893, when the opening salvos of this major economic depression hit. The first signs that the speculative bubble had begun to burst came in late 1892. In the latter half of that year and into the beginning of 1893, prices for staples such as breadstuffs, cotton, and iron began a steady decline, cutting into the profits of farmers and manufacturers. Railroads, including the colossal trans-continentals, began failing. Just days before the inauguration, the Philadelphia & Reading Railroad, whose stock plunged on news that its debt had climbed to a catastrophic $125 million, suddenly declared bankruptcy on February 26, and then the Erie railroad in July, Jay Gould's Northern Pacific in August, the Union Pacific in October, and the Atchison in December. In all, seventy major railroad lines, most of them with debt up to the hilt, went into receivership, a full 25 percent of all US rails. The shock caused alarm on Wall Street, which began seeing record stock sales.[11]

The overexpansion of railroads is a great example of the economic chaos during the 1890s, just as it had been in the 1870s. With all the new money floating around, particularly the massive subsidy program from governments on every level, railroads constructed 74,000 miles of new track during the decade of the 1880s, a record-breaking increase. The spurious building continued into the 1890s, though not necessarily out of the need to keep pace with an expanding economy but to keep pace with competing rail companies. Each railroad company, writes Professor Harold Faulkner, "recklessly and hastily threw up lines that were not needed, through miles and miles of uninhabited wilderness, merely to ensure that another road would not claim the territory first." The expansion, brought on in large part because of government interference, was too much for the economy to take, causing railroads to fail. With railroads going down, other industries inevitably followed, such as the vital manufacturing of steel. Ripples were spreading across the American economy.[12]

In early May, a major trust, the National Cordage Company, failed when its stock plummeted from $140 a share to $70. But the panic had just begun, and it would grow into one of the worst depressions of the nineteenth century and one of the most severe in American history.

Unemployment reached as high as eighteen and a half percent, caused by the failure of 15,242 businesses in 1893 alone, and another 13,905 in 1894, which was the highest rate since the downturn of the 1870s. In total, the panic saw the suspension, outright bankruptcy, or temporary closure of 575 banks, while the GNP fell by ten percent in two years.[13]

The situation was bad. Historian Henry Adams believed there was "nothing but universal bankruptcy before the world." He wrote that men "died like flies under the strain, and Boston grew suddenly old, haggard, and thin." Senator Shelby Cullom of Illinois noted, "The year 1893 closed with the prices of many products at the lowest ever known, with many workers seeking in vain for work, and with charity laboring to keep back suffering and starvation in all our cities." A young reporter in Chicago wrote home about what he saw in the Windy City. "There are thousands of homeless and starving men in the streets. I have seen more misery in this last week than I ever saw in my life before." The American correspondent for the *Bankers' Magazine* of London wrote that "ruin and disaster run riot over the land." The people of the United States were "in the throes of a fiasco unprecedented even in their broad experience." The country was on the verge of "a pronounced and serious panic."[14]

Though the economy was shrinking at an alarming rate, President Cleveland, who was supposedly in the pocket of big business, did nothing to help struggling companies and corporations with any direct government aid. He believed that everyone, individuals as well as businesses, should pull themselves up by their own bootstraps and not look to Washington for help. This was the commonly held economic view of his day, particularly for Jeffersonian Democrats. Congressman Michael D. Harter of Ohio reminded the nation that it was "not the business of the United States to raise prices, provide work, regulate wages, or in any way to interfere in the private business or personal affairs of the people." But some were beginning to believe the government could be a positive force in relieving people who were suffering through bad economic times. Senator James H. Berry of Arkansas was shocked that some members wanted to "be more liberal in appropriating money," simply "because times are hard," he said. "That is not my theory of the Constitution. My idea is that each individual citizen of the United States should look to himself, and it is not the purpose of this government to give work to individuals throughout the United States by appropriating money that belongs to other people and does not belong to the Senate."[15]

COMBATING INFLATION AND SAVING THE GOLD STANDARD

Instead of increasing the money supply, or worse still, increasing government spending as a solution, Cleveland focused on what he perceived as the real problem—the Sherman Silver Purchase Act of 1890, specifically its nefarious purchasing clause. He believed the only solution was for Congress to correct its mistake and rescind the bill. If not, Gresham's Law would come into play: "Bad money drives good money out of circulation." When too much cheap currency entered circulation, the nation's gold standard would be under threat, as people would hoard the more valuable coin, and that was exactly what was happening. This would place the nation on a de facto silver standard, the monetary system of the poorer nations of the world.

Yet the small but growing progressive wing of Cleveland's Democratic Party, as well as those in the Republican Party, believed the problem stemmed from a *scarcity* of money. In other words, they contended that there was a shortage of currency in circulation and that is what caused the contraction. A policy of inflation would benefit the poor by cheapening the dollars in circulation and making it easier to pay debts over time. This would greatly aid the lower classes, especially farmers.

In contrast to the progressive position, Cleveland saw the problem from the viewpoint of purchasing power, which would decrease as the currency increased. Every additional cheap dollar put into circulation caused the nation's money to lose value and caused the hoarding of gold. Should the nation continue to purchase 4.5 million ounces of silver a month, paying for it with treasury notes, and should the nation then enact a policy of free and unlimited coinage of silver, putting it into circulation, the results would have been disastrous. "I want a currency that is stable and safe in the hands of our people," Cleveland wrote to Governor W. J. Northen of Georgia, an advocate of free silver. "I will not knowingly be implicated in a condition that will make me in the least degree answerable to any laborer or farmer in the United States for a shrinkage in the purchasing power of the dollar he has received for a full dollar's worth of work or for a good dollar's worth of the product of his toil."[16]

In August 1893, Cleveland called Congress into special session to repeal the purchasing clause of the Sherman Silver Purchase Act. He sent a special message on the nation's financial situation and asked

Congress to rescind the law. The "alarming and extraordinary business situation," wrote the president, involves "the welfare and prosperity of all our people." The cause of the economic calamity was the continued "purchase and coinage of silver by the general government," a policy that has "made the depletion of our gold easy and have tempted other and more appreciative nations to add it to their stock." If the policy continued, the value of gold and silver "must part company" rather than remain in parity, which would cause the nation to lose its place "among nations of the first class" and deprive the people of "the best and safest money." Though he faced stiff resistance, on August 28, the House voted for repeal. The Senate followed suit but not until the end of October.[17]

Cleveland took overwhelming criticism for his leadership in seeking repeal, but stopping the inflation allowed the economy to begin to correct the imbalances within it. O. M. W. Sprague, who wrote a US Senate history of banking crises under the national banking system, noted that stopping the silver purchases "did much to restore confidence." Economist Murray Rothbard also believed that stopping the inflation helped bring an end to the panic by the end of 1893, as "foreign confidence rose with the Cleveland administration's successful repeal of the Sherman Silver Purchase Act," which saved the gold standard. Rothbard's analysis of the situation has been proven correct, as subsequent administrations held tightly to the gold standard and the economy eventually soared as a result.[18]

But Cleveland faced another problem as gold left the treasury at an alarming rate. To maintain a true gold standard, the federal government had to maintain a reserve of at least $100 million to back the amount of currency in circulation. That reserve was under threat. So, in an epic effort to stop the drain on the gold reserves, Cleveland decided to issue bonds, which could be purchased only in gold, in order to shore up the gold supply in the treasury. The president had the power to do this under existing law. In one bond sale, a group of major banking tycoons headed by J. P. Morgan bought most of them and turned a major profit in the process, which caused a flurry of protest, especially when it was discovered that Morgan had met with the president in the White House to discuss the merits of the plan. But Cleveland's deal, a use of the free-market financial system, helped save the gold standard and with it the American economy. Murray Rothbard, himself a libertarian of the Austrian school of economic thought, credited the "heroic" Cleveland-Morgan deal with restoring "confidence in the continuance of the gold standard."[19]

Though many wanted to keep the policy of inflation in place, and even increase the injection of silver and paper money into the economy to help the working classes, Cleveland stood strong against the tide. Critics hurled abuse at him daily. Henry Adams, an advocate for the poor and for free silver, even took to calling him "His Imperial Highness by God's Grace Grover the First." Many politicians in his own party shunned him. Progressive Democratic Governor John Altgeld of Illinois hurled a vicious attack at a Jefferson Day event. "To laud Clevelandism on Jefferson's birthday is to sing a *Te Deum* in honor of Judas Iscariot on a Christmas morning," he said. But none of the abuse bothered the president or kept him from doing what he knew to be the right thing, maintaining sound money at all costs. As biographer Allan Nevins has written, Cleveland's "greatest single service to the nation was ... his stubborn defense, against terrific assaults, of a sound financial system."[20]

CUTTING TAXES AND SHRINKING GOVERNMENT

After stopping the currency inflation and saving the gold standard, Cleveland turned his attention to the main source of federal revenue, the high protective tariff, operating at levels of fifty percent across the board, thanks to Bill McKinley's law in 1890. Taxes needed to be trimmed in order to help the economy recover, Cleveland believed, and he vowed to make it successful this time, especially since he now had a Democratic Congress.

But it wasn't the maintenance of party strength or the desire to keep his campaign pledges that stirred Cleveland to enact tariff reform. He had always believed the Republican protective tariff, in operation since 1861, was simply too high and in most cases brought in more revenue than the government needed. And with the sky-high McKinley Tariff, it began to reduce revenue, and with increased spending by the GOP, could cause deficits. That level of protection, Cleveland believed, was no longer necessary. As Cleveland argued during his first term, American industrial products dominated the world, there was no threat of foreign dumping, and the treasury had enough revenue to pay Washington's expenses, but only if Congress maintained the principles of economy in government. The high tariffs, then, looked to Cleveland like political payoffs to the main Republican special interest – Big Business. Reformer Carl Schurz called the high tariff "the greatest engine of political corruption on a grand scale that this country has ever seen." The *New York Times* agreed, referring to the Republican tariff act as the "McKinley abomination," to which every "monopolist and tax eater in the land ... has been pouring into the corruption fund of the Republican Party a part of the iniquitous tax he has been able to levy through Republican favor."[21]

Cleveland's main objective in tariff reform was to help the working classes receive lower prices on consumer goods. In the first annual message of his second term, sent to Congress on December 4, 1893, the president wrote that in order "to aid the people directly through tariff reform, one of its most obvious features should be a reduction in present tariff charges upon the necessaries of life. The benefits of such a reduction would be palpable and substantial, seen and felt by thousands who would be better fed and better clothed and better sheltered. These gifts should be the willing benefactions of a Government whose highest function is the promotion of the welfare of the people."[22]

On December 19, 1893, Congressman William L. Wilson, Chairman of the House Ways and Means Committee, who would later serve as Cleveland's postmaster general, rolled out a new tariff reform bill, which passed the House on February 1, 1894 by a significant margin, 204 to 140. Tariff duties were modestly cut by fifteen percent. However, to make up for any projected loss of revenue, the final House version of the bill included a provision for an income tax. The young Democratic congressman from Nebraska, William Jennings Bryan, introduced the tax amendment and vigorously defended it. "There is no more just tax upon the statute books than the income tax," he told the House.[23]

Though not a new concept, a tax on income was first enacted in the United States in 1862 to help finance Lincoln's War, and despite the Constitution's prohibition against direct taxes, federal courts left it alone as a war revenue measure. The original act created the Bureau of Internal Revenue, the forerunner to the IRS, to collect the tax. It covered all incomes of more than $600 a year at two graduated rates. Income greater than $600 and up to $10,000 was taxed at three percent, while everything greater than $10,000 was taxed at five percent. In 1864 the top rate was increased to ten percent. When applicable, the federal government had actually withheld the tax from people's income, such as government salaries, dividends and interest from bank stocks and bonds, as well as directly from corporations, like the massive railroad companies that receive subsidies from Washington. By the end of the war, some fifteen percent of households were paying the tax. In 1872 the law expired, and Republicans were content to leave it dead, as the tariff was continually pouring money into the federal treasury, making additional taxes unnecessary.[24]

The income tax of 1894 established a rate of just two percent on incomes of $4,000 or more, effectively exempting more than ninety-nine percent of the population. The two percent rate also applied to corporations, but those entities did not receive any exemption. So only the very rich would be affected by the new tax. With more than twelve million households across the nation, the tax would touch just 85,000 who had incomes of $4,000 or greater. This made the 1894 income tax much different in scope than its 1862 predecessor. "For the first time in American history," writes economic historian John Steele Gordon, "a tax was seemingly proposed on a particular class of citizens, a class defined by economic success." Critics used this feature to attack the tax proposal as "socialism." Cleveland's fellow New Yorker and longtime political antagonist, Senator David B. Hill, blamed the tax on "little squads of anarchists, communists, and socialists" from Europe infecting America with foreign ideas.[25]

But supporters pointed to the massive concentration of wealth to make their case. "The tax proposed on incomes," wrote former Congressman Roger Q. Mills in its defense, "is but a light touch on the monumental piles of wealth, for the protection of which the government is standing guard." Mills argued that continued wealth accumulation might lead to "an upheaval" not unlike that of revolutionary France in 1789 when the clergy and nobility "persistently refused to bear any burden of taxation to support the government."[26]

Thomas G. Shearman, a political economist and founder of the Shearman and Sterling Law Firm in New York City, conducted a study on the concentration of wealth in America, which he published in 1889 in *The Forum* under the title "The Owners of the United States of America." Shearman contended that just seventy persons owned a combined wealth of $2.7 billion. Some fifty thousand families owned half the nation's wealth, while four-fifths of the people earned less than

$500 a year. Although he represented such prominent American figures as Jay Gould, Henry Ford, and John D. Rockefeller and his Standard Oil giant, Shearman supported an income tax "upon rents and corporations having exclusive privileges." The current tax burden with the high tariff, Shearman noted, was disproportionately placed upon the poor, who paid taxes equivalent to seventy-five to eighty percent of their savings while corporations and the wealthy paid only eight to ten percent. Federal taxes had increased six-fold since the war, while untaxed corporations saw their profits soar tenfold. This had to change, he contended.[27]

As a strong Jeffersonian, Cleveland had his own reservations. He had discussed the great disparity of wealth in his final annual message in 1888, and had given his support for "a small tax upon incomes derived from certain corporate investments." His proposal was certainly not an income tax in the traditional sense and would, in no way, touch the lower classes but would resemble modern-day capital gains taxes, first instituted in 1913, and tax the massive corporations that paid almost no taxes yet stood protected behind an enormous tariff wall. But this proposal by Congressman Bryan was essentially wealth redistribution, something Cleveland would never support.[28]

The president also had another reason to look on the income tax with suspicion. Not only did it violate a fundamental principle of Jeffersonian economic thought, it gave Congress additional funds to spend. "The income tax became the fuel for paternalism in government," writes tax historian Charles Adams, "just as excises and land and wealth taxes had done in Europe centuries before." Cleveland understood this and certainly did not want to see government paternalism expand any further. But many wanted to see a tariff reform act, any tariff reform act, become law. Even the *New York Times* desired passage, even though it contained "the obnoxious income tax amendment." With a complete Democratic government for the first time since James Buchanan's administration, this might be their only hope.[29]

Chairman Wilson privately opposed inclusion of the tax, mainly because he feared it would upset Cleveland. In fact, the president wrote him that he "deprecated the incorporation in the proposed bill of the income tax feature," primarily because it was a major distraction from the real issue before Congress, that of tariff reform. According to Josephus Daniels, private secretary to the Interior Secretary Hoke Smith, it was

"Bryan who forced the income tax provision in the Wilson Tariff Act. Mr. Cleveland, Mr. Carlisle [Treasury Secretary], and Mr. Wilson did not wish it incorporated in the tariff measure." In the end, however, Wilson relented to the pressure, and the income tax amendment passed by a vote of 182 to 48. The whole tax package was then sent to the Senate, where it faced an uncertain future in what many in the House considered an "aristocratic club of millionaires."[30]

As with the repeal of the Sherman Silver Purchase Act, the Senate dragged its feet on the tariff reform bill – not for the purpose of slowing down the process by procedure but in order to rewrite the entire bill. Cleveland was again aggravated by the actions of the Senate, calling their activities a "deadly blight of treason." Leading the effort to make the bill into the Senate's image was Maryland Democratic Senator Arthur Pue Gorman, joined by David B. Hill of New York and James Smith Jr. of New Jersey, along with three other Democrats, who united with the opposition Republicans, who would not tolerate any tampering with its signature policy of protection.[31]

With Gorman leading the charge, no one in the administration could have a shred of confidence that things would turn out well. The bill "had the bad fortune to be in the hands of Senator Gorman," wrote Josephus Daniels. "He was one of the most astute men in public life, a straight party man, but he had no zeal for reform or righteousness." Every Senator "who wanted a little graft was accommodated." In the control of protectionists, the Upper Chamber considered the issue of tariff reform for five months, tacking on 634 amendments to the House bill that hiked tariff rates on a host of articles. Most senators wanted to protect the interests of their respective states. Louisiana's Senate delegation vowed not to support any deal unless a duty was placed on imported sugar from Cuba. Senator Stephen White of California sought duties on imported fruit. Senators from coal and iron ore states wanted those items imported from foreign nations taxed as well.[32]

Both sides – Cleveland and the reformers on one and Gorman and the protectionists on the other – dug in and battled throughout the spring. Historians have generally portrayed the years between Lincoln's War and the Spanish-American War of 1898 as relatively quiet. But one veteran Washington journalist, David S. Barry, noted that the fight over the Wilson Tariff Bill "literally set the country on fire," stirring "the people into a frenzy of political discussion." Because of the president's staunch anti-silver stand, the animosity between Cleveland and many Senate Democrats was already strong; the tariff fight soured their already weakened relationship further. Senator John Morgan of Alabama professed to hate the very ground the president walked on. Not exactly a climate conducive to conducting the nation's business.[33]

Despite the political rancor, the reform bill, now dubbed the Wilson-Gorman Tariff Bill, passed in the Senate on July 3 by a close vote of 39 to 34, with a dozen Senators abstaining from the vote. Raw materials on the free list dwindled to just two: wool and copper. Tariffs were raised on iron, wool and cotton products, glass, certain chemicals, and sugar, both raw and refined. The income tax amendment also remained. But because of the vast differences between the two proposals, it would be left up to a House-Senate conference committee to determine the final outcome.[34]

Cleveland had high hopes for a good bill emerging from the conference committee. It would "present the best, if not the only, hope of true Democracy," the president wrote Wilson in a letter read on the House floor, "and the redemption of Democratic promises to the people." The Senate bill "falls far short of the consummation for which we have long labored, for which we have suffered defeat without discouragement," and should the effort be abandoned, it would mean "party perfidy and party dishonor." The final bill, Cleveland insisted, must include the free importation of raw materials if it is to "bear a genuine Democratic badge" and be of any help to the people.[35]

But rather than work out a compromise, the House decided to accept the Senate's version, which included the income tax provision. On August 13, the House passed the Senate's bill by a vote of 182 to 105, despite Wilson's noble effort to prevent it. In the end the final bill lowered rates from fifty to forty-two percent. Cleveland was so disgusted with the process that he allowed the bill to become law without his signature. He hated the income tax provision and detested the Senate's action on the original bill, but he did favor the small cut in taxes.

As he had in his 1888 message, he went after the wealthy and their influence over the proposed tariff legislation. It was "the trusts and combinations – the communism of pelf – whose machinations have prevented us from reaching the success we deserved," he wrote Mississippi Congressman Thomas C. Catchings. The tariff law, though flawed, "presents a vast improvement to existing conditions" and lightens "many tariff burdens that now rest heavily upon the people. It is not only a barrier against the return of mad protection, but it furnishes a vantage-ground from which must be waged further aggressive operations against protected monopoly and governmental favoritism." This bill was a step in the right direction, he contended, but because it had provisions "which are not in line with honest tariff reform," with "inconsistencies and crudities which ought not to appear in tariff laws or laws of any kind," like the income tax, he did not sign it.[36]

But Cleveland had good reason to believe the Supreme Court, in a time of very conservative justices who saw themselves as guardians of the Constitution, would not allow the income tax to remain in place. During his first term in 1888, he appointed Melville Fuller, a resolute Jeffersonian, as Chief Justice. Fuller was arguably the best Chief Justice in American history, ruling on many serious constitutional questions, including the Sherman Antitrust Act, and always upholding the original intent of the Founders. Unsurprisingly, the Fuller Court struck down the income tax provision as an unconstitutional direct tax in 1895 in *Pollock v. Farmers' Loan & Trust Co* by a 5 to 4 vote. It would not be until the advent of the Sixteenth Amendment, ratified in 1913, that the country would have a permanent tax on incomes.[37]

Like Jefferson, President Cleveland also cut spending during his second term. Although some wanted to spend more money as the economy slowed, that was not possible with a Jeffersonian president. He urged restraint. "At this time, when a depleted public Treasury confronts us," he told Congress, "when many of our people are engaged in a hard struggle for the necessities of life, and when enforced economy is pressing upon the great mass of our countrymen, I desire to urge with all the earnestness at my command that Congressional legislation be so limited by strict economy as to exhibit an appreciation of the condition of the Treasury and a sympathy with the straitened circumstances of our fellow citizens." When he took over for Harrison, the federal budget was at $383 million, which he trimmed to $352 million by 1896, his final full year in office.[38]

And what were the results of these free-market measures? After the loss of ten percent of GNP in two years, the economy began to grow in 1895, making up the losses and gaining an additional twenty percent by

1897 from its low point in 1894. Unemployment was a bit more sluggish, dropping from eighteen and a half percent in 1894 to fourteen and a half by 1897, but by 1900 it was at just five percent. The quick turnaround has caused economists and historians to erroneously categorize it as no worse than a minor recession, but the Panic of 1893 had the potential to be the worst economic calamity in American history. But because Cleveland used free-market principles instead of socialistic intervention, the crisis was short-lived.[39]

THE REPUBLICAN "BLAME GAME"

The panic did have an unfortunate consequence: It quickly ended Grover Cleveland's second Jeffersonian interlude. With the depression striking just as conservative Democrats took power, they received all the blame, even though the party had nothing to do with the policies that had caused it. Beginning in 1888, with the election of Harrison, Republicans held the government and, most importantly, put into place their policies of inflation and increased spending, fiscal programs that caused the downturn by making an already bad financial bubble much worse. The economy soon went into a correction because of a disproportionate amount of inflation from both the Sherman Silver Purchase Act and the ramped-up expenditures.

Naturally, Republicans pounced on Cleveland for the downturn. In his memoirs, Senator John Sherman, a former Treasury Secretary and younger brother of the famous Union general, held Cleveland responsible for the depression, even though he had not been in power for four years when the downturn struck. Nevertheless, Sherman argued that the *anticipation* of more conservative policies caused the crash. For Senator Sherman, whose name graced the silver purchase law, it was Cleveland's election that "created the disturbances that followed it. The fear of radical changes in the tariff law was the basis of them." Sherman even claimed that he only loaned his name to the bill, which he argued was only a compromise hatched in order to prevent the free and unlimited coinage of silver. He objected to the silver purchases and to the issuance of the new treasury notes, stating that he "had foreseen this inevitable result" of economic depression. Cleveland had been saying the same thing all throughout his first term but received no credit for his repeated warnings.[40]

Despite the persistent criticism from Republicans, President Cleveland did receive some praise from members of the opposition party. He did what he believed was right to correct the economic depression that struck the nation in 1893 and demonstrated, according to Republican Chauncey M. Depew, "an extraordinary degree of courage and steadfastness." Senator William B. Allison, an Iowa Republican and the coauthor of the Bland-Allison Silver Act of 1878, also credited Cleveland for having the audacity to repeal the Sherman Act. It was God's mercy that Cleveland was elected in 1892, Allison told Horace White of the *New York Evening Post*, for no Republican "could have procured the repeal ... however strongly he might have tried." No Democrat other than Cleveland could have been successful either, and had the president failed to get the bill repealed, "we should now be a ruined people." This was quite a compliment coming from a man who was so knowledgeable on economic matters that two presidents, Chester Arthur and Benjamin Harrison, asked him to serve as Secretary of the Treasury, offers he declined.[41]

Progressives in both parties had sown the seeds of depression, but unfortunately, Cleveland Democrats reaped the rotten fruit. Unsurprisingly, with the Republican campaign of blaming the Democrats, the public laid the blame at the feet of those in power. In the midterm elections in 1894, Cleveland's party was decimated, losing control of both houses of Congress. Two years later, in 1896, the party lost the presidency to William McKinley, even though the economy was finally beginning to rebound. The economy had suffered through three years of depression, which was not Cleveland's fault. He put in place the policies to get the nation moving again but the seemingly never-ending agitation over free silver held down economic growth. With the business community not knowing what type of monetary policy the nation would have, it caused what economists refer to as "regime uncertainty." The great economic growth enjoyed by President McKinley had little to do with his legislative program, save his market-calming adherence to the gold standard, but had more to do with the free market economic policies enacted by Grover Cleveland.

In an interesting factoid of American history, many financial panics were presided over by Presidents who had been New York governors – Martin Van Buren and the Panic of 1837, Cleveland and the Panic of 1893, Theodore Roosevelt and the Panic of 1907, and Franklin Roosevelt and the Great Depression of the 1930s. But Cleveland's story has a unique twist to it, one involving Van Buren and a young FDR.

Cleveland was born in 1837, the year of the worst financial panic to strike the young nation, presided over by President Van Buren, a former New York governor. Cleveland, also hailing from New York and serving as the state's governor, would, as we have seen, preside over the Panic of 1893, which rivaled 1837's in its severity and could easily have eclipsed it.

While president, Cleveland met the young son of one of his New York supporters, a five-year-old lad named Franklin Delano Roosevelt, who came to the White House with his father, James, a strong Cleveland man whom the president wanted to appoint as minister to Holland, a position the elder Roosevelt respectfully declined. President Cleveland, by then exacerbated by all the work he faced and the constant throng of office-seekers, placed his hand on young Franklin's head and said, "My little man, I am making a strange wish for you. It is that you may never be president of the United States." But the young man would indeed become president nearly fifty years later, after two terms as the governor of New York, and preside over the nation's worst economic depression, a panic that surpassed both 1837 and 1893 in its severity. Yet Van Buren and Cleveland treated their respective calamities much differently than FDR and had much better results, even though establishment historians rarely given them the credit they deserve.[42]

Endnotes

1   Irwin Unger, *The Greenback Era: A Social and Political History of American Finance, 1865-1879* (Princeton: Princeton University Press, 1964), 15-6.

2   Kermit L. Hall, ed., *The Oxford Companion to the Supreme Court of the United States* (New York: Oxford University Press, 1992), 685, 498-9; Sidney Ratner, "Was the Supreme Court Packed by President Grant?" *Political Science Quarterly* (September 1935): 343-58.

3   Milton Friedman, "The Crime of 1873" *Journal of Political Economy* (December 1990): 1159-94.

4   Ray B. Westerfield, *Our Silver Debacle* (New York: The Ronald Press Company, 1936), 7; Unger, 81, 89-91.

5   Several economists, such as Murray Rothbard, have conclusively proven that there was no economic depression after the panic. Historians and some economists, citing deflation, have long argued that a depression lasted until 1879 but the economy, as well as the money supply, greatly expanded during that period. See Rothbard, *A History of Money and Banking in the United States*, 154-5.

6   John Sherman, *Recollections of Forty Years*, 2 volumes (Chicago: The Werner Company, 1895), II, 1187; Welch, 128.

7   Rothbard, *History*, 168.

8   Henry Villard, *Memoirs of Henry Villard, Journalist and Financier, 1835-1900*, 2 volumes. (Boston: Houghton, Mifflin and Company, 1904), II, 357-9.

9   Nevins, *Cleveland*, 525; Stanley Lebergott, *Manpower in Economic Growth: The American Record Since 1800* (New York: McGraw-Hill, 1964), 522; Carter, *Historical Statistics*, IV, 80-1; John Steele Gordon, *Hamilton's Blessing: The Extraordinary Life and Times of Our National Debt* (New York: Walker & Company, 2010), 85.

10   Benjamin Harrison, Fourth Annual Message to Congress, December 6, 1892, Richardson, ed., *Messages and Papers*, XII, 5741, 5744; Carl Schurz, "Cleveland's Second Administration," in Frederic Bancroft, ed., *Speeches, Correspondence and Political Papers of Carl Schurz*, 6 volumes (New York: G. P. Putnam's Sons, 1913), IV, 347.

11   Nevins, *Cleveland,* 525; *Wall Street Journal,* May 5, 1893; Harold U. Faulkner, *Politics, Reform and Expansion, 1890-1900* (New York: Harper & Row, Publishers, 1959), 141; *Wall Street Journal,* February 27, 1893.

12   Faulkner, 145.

13   Charles A. Collman, *Our Mysterious Panics, 1830-1930* (New York: Greenwood Press, 1968), 161; Lebergott, 522; Carter, *Historical Statistics,* III, 550, 24-5; O. M. W. Sprague, *History of Crises under the National Banking System* (Washington: Government Printing Office, 1910), 400-3.

14   Henry Adams, *The Education of Henry Adams* (Boston: Houghton Mifflin Company, 1918), 338; Cullom, 264; R. Hal Williams, *Years of Decision: American Politics in the 1890s* (New York: John Wiley & Sons, 1978), 77; *Bankers' Magazine* of London, September 1893, as quoted in Samuel Rezneck, *Business Depressions and Financial Panics* (New York: Greenwood Press, 1968), 324.

15   Robert Higgs, *Crisis and Leviathan: Critical Episodes in the Growth of American Government* (New York: Oxford University Press, 1987), 86.

16   Cleveland to Governor W. J. Northern, September 25, 1893, Nevins, *Letters,* 335-6.

17   Cleveland, Special Session Message, August 8, 1893, Richardson, ed., *Messages and Papers,* XII, 5833-5837.

18   Sprague, 208; Rothbard, 169.

19   Rothbard, 169.

20   Olasky, 164; Nevins, *Cleveland,* 201.

21   Carl Schurz, "The Issues of the National Campaign of 1892," September 18, 1892, *Papers of Schurz,* IV, 100; *New York Times,* January 31, 1894.

22   Cleveland, First Annual Message to Congress, December 4, 1893, Richardson, ed., *Messages and Papers,* XII, 5866-92.

23   John Sharp Williams to Davie Crompton, February 14, 1894, John Sharp Williams Papers, Mississippi Department of Archives and History, Jackson, MS; Welch, 132-3; William Jennings Bryan, Speech on the Income Tax, House of Representatives, January 30, 1894, *Speeches of William Jennings Bryan* (New York: Funk & Wagnalls Company, 1909), 164.

24   Hummel, *Freeing Slaves,* 223; Gordon, *Hamilton's Blessing,* 70-1; Charles Adams, *Those Dirty Rotten Taxes: The Tax Revolts that Built America* (New York: The Free Press, 1998), 141.

25   Higgs, 99; Adams, *Dirty Rotten Taxes*, 141; Gordon, *Hamilton's Blessing*, 80; Charles Adams, *For Good and Evil: The Impact of Taxes on the Course of Civilization* (Lanham, Maryland: Madison Books, 1999), 364.

26   Roger Q. Mills, "The Wilson Bill," *North American Review* (February, 1894), 237–8; Weisman, 122–3.

27   Thomas G. Shearman to Roger Q. Mills, June 12, 1893, Mills Papers, Dallas Historical Society, Dallas, TX.

28   Cleveland, First Annual Message to Congress, December 4, 1893, Richardson, ed., *Messages and Papers*, XII, 5866–92.

29   Adams, *Dirty Rotten Taxes*, 131, *New York Times*, January 31, 1894.

30   Cleveland to Wilson, July 2, 1894, Nevins, *Letters*, 357; Josephus Daniels, *Editor in Politics* (Chapel Hill: University of North Carolina Press, 1941), 76; Nevins, *Cleveland*, 565; John Sharp Williams to Davie Crompton, February 14, 1894, John Sharp Williams Papers, Mississippi Department of Archives and History, Jackson, MS.

31   Cullom, 265; Schurz, "Second Administration," 361. The "deadly blight of treason" comment can be found in Cleveland to Thomas C. Catchings, August 27, 1894, Thomas C. Catchings Papers, Tulane. This letter can also be found in Nevins, *Letters*, 364–6.

32   Daniels, *Editor in Politics*, 74; Welch, 134.

33   Barry, 193, Nevins, *Cleveland*, 568.

34   Welch, 134.

35   Cleveland to Wilson, July 2, 1894, Nevins, *Letters*, 354–7.

36   Cleveland to Catchings, August 27, 1894, Catchings Papers, Tulane.

37   Keller, 308; Lawrence W. Reed, "A Supreme Court to Be Proud Of," The Freeman, March 2006, http://www.thefreemanonline.org/columns/ideas-and-consequences-a-supreme-court-to-be-proud-of/.

38   Cleveland, First Annual Message to Congress, December 4, 1893, Richardson, ed., *Messages and Papers*, XII, 5866–92; Carter, *Historical Statistics*, V, 80–1.

39   Carter, *Historical Statistics*, III, 24–5; Lebergott, 522.

40   Sherman, *Recollections*, II, 1207.

41   Chauncey M. Depew, *My Memories of Eighty Years* (New York: Charles Scribner's Sons, 1924), 127; Horace White to Cleveland, April 16, 1894, Nevins, *Letters*, 350.

42   Jean Edward Smith, *FDR* (New York: Random House, 2008), 23.

Chapter 5

How Cleveland's Foreign Policy Upheld Jeffersonian Traditions

"I am for free commerce with all nations, political connection with none, and little or no diplomatic establishment. And I am not for linking ourselves by new treaties with the quarrels of Europe, entering that field of slaughter to preserve their balance, or joining in the confederacy of Kings to war against the principles of liberty."

—Thomas Jefferson to Elbridge Gerry, January 26, 1799

"The genius of our institutions ... dictate the scrupulous avoidance of any departure from that foreign policy commended by the history, the traditions, and the prosperity of our Republic. It is the policy of neutrality, rejecting any share in foreign broils and ambitions upon other continents and repelling their intrusion here."

—President Grover Cleveland, First Inaugural Address, March 4, 1885.

For most of the nineteenth century, American foreign policy took a back seat to more pressing domestic concerns, like sectional conflict and slavery expansion during the 1850s and 1860s, and later with issues like industrialization and immigration in the 1870s and 1880s. All that began to change, though, as the century came to a close. America moved slowly into the realm of a world power, and overseas affairs became more prominent. But, with these changes, what should be the role of the United States in world affairs? It is a question asked throughout American history, in Grover Cleveland's time as well as our own.

JEFFERSONIAN FOREIGN POLICY

America's traditional foreign policy model came out of the Jefferson administration. In his Inaugural Address in 1801, President Jefferson announced his intention to promote peace, commerce, and honest friendship with all nations but to steer clear of "entangling alliances." Washington had said much the same thing in his farewell address in September 1796, warning of the dangers of a permanent alliance system, but the Jeffersonians wanted no alliances and clearly sought to remain as neutral and as isolationist as possible, making no promises that could involve the nation in a foreign war. As president, Jefferson withdrew many US ambassadors from their overseas posts as being unnecessary. But American ideals ran much deeper than simply recalling diplomats and staying out of the business of other nations. In the Declaration of Independence, Jefferson enunciated the principle of self-determination of peoples, which guided US foreign policy for more than a century.

President Cleveland echoed similar sentiments in both inaugural addresses, as well as in his annual messages and public speeches. The "spirit of fairness and love of justice," he wrote in his annual message in 1893, as well as "consistent fairness, characterize a truly American foreign policy." He would never use diplomacy or the American military for anything other than national or hemispheric defense and certainly not for gaining new territories in distant lands, as the powers of Europe were then doing. He took Jefferson to heart.[1]

But the attitudes of those in government, as well as many across the country, were changing as the turn of the century dawned. The same forces of progressivism that sought a more activist government at home also wanted a more forward-looking foreign policy abroad. Cleveland would fight the same progressive influences over the nation's foreign affairs, just as he battled the forces of progressivism in domestic policy. Progressives sought to change society, hopefully for the better, to make people conform to a certain set of behaviors, and to use government for the possible perfectibility of mankind and human civilization. Though we tend to think of it in terms of domestic policy, the progressive agenda also reached its tentacles across the continent and around the globe to begin the same process in alien lands. The notion of imperialism is simply progressivism applied abroad. Many of the better-known progressives, such as Theodore Roosevelt and Woodrow Wilson, believed in foreign adventurism. But Cleveland hated it as much as he detested the vast changes being proposed at home.[2]

MAINTAINING A STRONG NATIONAL DEFENSE

Not favoring an internationalist foreign policy did not mean that Cleveland preferred a weak military. Rather, he presided over a buildup of the US Navy, creating a nucleus that eventually made it one of the best in the world. In those days, before the advent of air power and nuclear weapons, naval forces were the weapons of choice and indicative of a modern power. In the late nineteenth century, the American Navy grew into a force that easily defeated the Spanish in 1898 and helped Teddy Roosevelt exert American influence around the globe, although that was never Cleveland's intention.

The naval buildup had actually begun under his predecessor, Chester Arthur, who earned the moniker "Father of the Modern Navy," but the modernization was greatly increased under Cleveland. He saw the navy's value as a defender of the nation and the hemisphere in more troubled times, so he approved each naval appropriation bill that Congress passed, particularly large measures in 1886 and 1887. Under the watchful eye of Navy Secretary William Whitney, the fleet added 93,951 tons of new ships, compared to 11,986 tons during Arthur's administration. Whitney made sure the new steel vessels, which would replace the twenty-six wooden ships still in service, were constructed from American sources and not from foreign suppliers. Thus, Cleveland was just as responsible as his predecessor for the buildup of the great modern steel navy that was so vital to national defense well into the twentieth century.[3]

NEW IMPERIALISM

While the United States maintained a more isolationist foreign policy for most of the nineteenth century, the powers of Europe were expanding around the globe, acquiring colonies in every corner. This great revival of Western expansion, called the New Imperialism, ran from around 1870 until 1914 and is somewhat surprising in that during most of the preceding century, imperialism had been widely seen as a fiscally unsound endeavor by most European statesmen. Yet the New Imperialism was an explosion of Western conquest that would far exceed the achievements of the Age of Discovery in the fifteenth century. It was the beginning of a new era, the Age of Empire.

The main justification behind the New Imperialism was racism—or to be more precise, scientific racism. These theories, put forward by leading scientists across Europe, including Charles Darwin, held that inferior races needed guidance and supervision from superior peoples. Britain led the way in this new way of thinking. Cecil Rhodes, an English imperialist in Africa who had large stakes in gold and diamond mining, and also served as Prime Minister of the Cape Colony from 1890–96, advised Britain to seize as much territory as possible. "We are the finest race in the world," he boasted, "and the more of the world we inhabit, the better it is for the human race." He even once told a reporter that he would annex the planets if he could.[4]

Following in Rhodes's footsteps, English author Rudyard Kipling wrote a poem called "The White Man's Burden" in 1899, where he advocated imperialism. He wrote in part:

> Take up the white man's burden
> Send forth the best ye breed
> Go bind your sons to exile
> To serve your captives' need;
> To wait in heavy harness
> On fluttered folk and wild
> Your new-caught, sullen peoples,
> Half devil and half child.

To Kipling, third-world nations were uncivilized and childlike, and the superior races in the West had a moral obligation to introduce them to Christianity, modern education systems, and technological advancements that flowed out of "superior" Western nations. There was no way such backward peoples could go it alone, it was widely believed.[5]

As these debates raged in Europe, Americans began seeing themselves as a special people and an exceptional nation. One US senator stated in 1893, "We are sixty-five million of people, the most advanced and powerful on earth." Another believed the nation should expand throughout all of

North and Central America. The "northern boundary must be the Arctic Circle and our southern boundary the Isthmus Canal," he said. Such thinking was derisively termed by its detractors as "jingoism," usually defined as an expression of extreme patriotism and the advocacy of an aggressive foreign policy to achieve territorial aspirations, a new "manifest destiny" but at a much higher level.[6]

Such boisterous statements by politicians were certainly not on the lips of everyone, as numerous Americans believed the prevailing jingoism to be "absolutely crazy," to quote one critic. Yet more and more were coming to believe the United States had been given a special mission in the world and could be as great as the powers of Europe, if it were not already so. But Europe was in the process of acquiring colonies, engaged heavily in a "scramble for Africa" and in attaining "spheres of influence" in Asia, while the United States risked falling behind the world's leaders. If it wanted to keep up, and truly be one of the most powerful nations on Earth, then American foreign policy had to change.[7]

In 1890, American naval officer Captain Alfred Thayer Mahan, a professor at the Naval War College, wrote one of antiquity's most important books, *The Influence of Sea Power upon History*, which argued that naval power is the key component that made nations strong. Britain, Mahan reminded his readers, dominated the world and its commerce because of its powerful navy, which allowed it to control the sea-lanes, protect its merchant fleet, and, in time of war, blockade an enemy's ports. Despite its recent naval buildup, the United States possessed naval vessels that were lacking in technological advancement, far behind the forces of other great naval powers. He contended that America should abandon its policy of continental and hemispheric defense and build a truly modern blue-water naval force that could be used for offensive warfare around the globe. He also advocated the acquisition of territory for bases and refueling stops, all in order to become one of the great powers of the world. This significant work was an international bestseller, widely read even by the great statesmen of the world. Kaiser Wilhelm II shifted German naval strategy after reading it, which helped pave the way for World War One. More importantly, the book greatly influenced future American leaders like Teddy Roosevelt, who would transform American foreign policy into a more aggressive strategy.[8]

Mahan's thinking fell in line with the outlook of many fellow jingoistic Americans, like Roosevelt, his good friend Senator Henry Cabot Lodge, and others in and out of government, who saw war as a good thing, a healthy and cleansing process for the nation. It was a strange concept for a country that was only one generation removed from the bloodiest war of the nineteenth century and the worst in the entire history of the Western Hemisphere. But many up-and-coming leaders, like TR, had been small children in the 1860s and had no real memory of the conflict between the North and South. The torch was being passed to a new generation of Americans who would take foreign policy in a new direction and away from self-determination for all peoples.

OPPOSITION TO NATION BUILDING

Cleveland did not buy into the jingoist and imperialist arguments, or in the suggestion that America needed a larger global naval force than what it was then building. Unlike many jingoists, he remembered the great sectional conflict and never believed war was anything but bad. Soon after retaking office in 1893 to begin his second term, Cleveland faced a serious test of American foreign policy in a situation concerning the Hawaiian Islands and the role the United States played in a recent revolution there.

Hawaii remained an independent nation in the early 1890s, ruled by a native monarch. But the islands were in the process of undergoing major demographic changes, as native Hawaiians died out and were replaced with foreigners, namely Europeans and Americans, but also laborers from China and Japan. The natives were holding on but by a thread only. A native population of 200,000 in 1800 had been reduced to 40,000 by 1890, with disease causing a major portion of the decline. The foreign population also swelled, with nearly 30,000 Japanese and Chinese, 9,000 Portuguese, and 2,000 Americans, the major group that dominated the economy. But the Japanese population was growing fast.[9]

The economy of the islands centered heavily on sugar production, with the major plantations being under the thumb of non-Hawaiians, mostly Americans. A small cabal of wealthy white families, known as "Outlanders," so-named after an influx of European settlers, effectively controlled the economy and with it the government and all of Hawaiian society. By the early 1890s, the natives still held the monarchy, which served as the titular head of the government, but was, in actuality, merely a figurehead. Real power centered in the parliament, controlled by the Outlanders.[10]

In the United States, progressive Republicans began pushing a much more aggressive foreign policy. After conquering the South by crushing the Confederacy, and the West by subjugating the Plains Indians, Republicans turned their attention from wars of subjugation at home and looked farther to the west at the Asian realm in this new bout of jingoism. They began casting an envious eye on the lucrative and strategically located island chain. Jeffersonian, non-interventionist Democrats did not fall into line. President John Tyler, an old Southern Democrat, had extended the Monroe Doctrine over the islands in the 1840s but left it at that. After the War Between the States, as foreign-led annexationist movements spread on the islands, President Andrew Johnson, another old Democrat, announced that a treaty had been negotiated that would allow Hawaii to "voluntarily apply for admission to the Union." But progressive Republicans in Congress rejected the voluntary offer. They wanted Hawaii by right, if not outright force. The inferior Hawaiians should have no say in the matter. In 1881, President James Garfield announced that the United States should be the "arbiter" of the Pacific, as well as "the controller of its commerce and chief nation that inhabits its shores," which included the Hawaiian Islands.[11]

By that time, the federal government had already become officially involved with Hawaii. Republican President Ulysses S. Grant and his Secretary of State, Hamilton Fish, negotiated a reciprocity treaty in 1875 that would, in Fish's words, "bind these islands to the United States with hoops of steel." The economic agreement allowed the island's major crop of sugar to enter the American market duty-free. Likewise, US products could enter the Hawaiian market free of charge. The treaty proved prosperous for both nations, though Hawaii had become, more or less, an "economic colony" of the United States with 99 percent of its products sent to the American market, mainly sugar. This was Fish's whole intent. In 1887, during Cleveland's first term, the two governments renewed the trade agreement, but the Senate amended the original treaty to give the United States exclusive rights to a naval base at the mouth of the Pearl River, which would become Pearl Harbor. Cleveland, along with Secretary of State Thomas Bayard, was instrumental in negotiating this provision.[12]

Cleveland believed in the vitality of Hawaii for economic and military purposes only, and he agreed with Republicans on the need for trade and commerce, but he did not hold their nationalistic views on annexation, which would have destroyed Hawaiian sovereignty, always a strong progressive goal. He favored annexation, but only if native Hawaiians, through true self-determination, desired it. If not, his policy was only to uphold the Monroe Doctrine and protect the islands against outside influences. In 1887, he blocked the British from offering a loan of $2 million to Hawaii. Though it might have seemed innocent on the outside, Cleveland understood what the British were up to. In exchange for the loan, the English government asked for a share of Hawaiian revenue as collateral. This would have put the British Lion squarely in the middle of Hawaiian affairs, a clear violation of the Monroe Doctrine. That he would not allow.[13]

The federal government had every reason to want, in the least, to maintain the status quo in Hawaii. If the islands could not be annexed, they should remain an economic colony. When Benjamin Harrison became president in 1889, following Cleveland's first term, he ordered the landing of seventy marines from the *USS Adams* to prevent a coup against the weak monarch, King Kalakaua. Harrison also mandated a permanent US naval presence in the area. But in 1891 the situation changed dramatically and threatened to overturn the status quo. A new native monarch came to the throne, a headstrong, highly nationalistic woman named Liliuokalani, sister to King Kalakaua, who had died of an illness. She desired to run Hawaii herself with a program of "Hawaii for Hawaiians." She wanted to diminish the influence of the Outlanders if not outright end it, and she proposed a new constitution that stripped all non-Hawaiians of the right to vote. Her proposal threatened the existing power structure, then in the hands of the major planters.[14]

The Outlanders had to do something about the new, impulsive queen. On the night of January 14, 1893, the US minister to Hawaii, John Stevens, met secretly with a group plotting the queen's overthrow, a faction known as the "Annexation Club." Though Harrison and his jingoistic Secretary of State, James G. Blaine, denied any knowledge of the coup, it is likely that both knew of the plan and did nothing to discourage it. When the queen announced the new constitution, the scheme was launched, apparently by orders from Stevens himself, who happened to be a benefactor, business partner, and close friend of Blaine's. A US warship, the *USS*

Boston, supplied American troops to assist in the revolt by keeping order, an important task in any successful coup. The plotters removed the queen without bloodshed and established a provisional government under the protection of US forces. Native Hawaiians were stripped of the right to vote, giving full control to the Outlanders.[15]

Stevens immediately recognized the provisional government. Unsurprisingly, the new provisional authority asked for annexation to the United States, and the American flag began flying over Hawaiian government buildings. "The Hawaiian pear is now fully ripe, and this is the golden hour for the United States to pluck it," Minister Stevens announced. President Harrison wholeheartedly agreed, calling the Hawaiian monarchy "weak" and "inadequate." Secretary of State Blaine drew up a treaty to annex the Hawaiian Islands, which the president submitted to the Senate.[16]

The treaty remained in the Senate when President Cleveland came back into office on March 4, 1893, just two months after the coup. He did not like the manner in which the queen had been overthrown or that the United States minister and American forces had been involved, which he felt caused "serious embarrassment" for the country. To get a handle on events, Cleveland named James H. Blount, a twenty-year veteran of Congress from Georgia, as a commissioner to Hawaii for the purpose of discovering exactly what had transpired. Blount spent four months investigating and found a military protectorate in the hands of US troops, which were even conducting regular police duties for the provisional government, as if American forces were under their control. He also discovered that a majority of Hawaiians did not favor annexation. In July he filed a report on his findings.[17]

The Blount investigation showed "beyond all question that the constitutional Government of Hawaii had been subverted with the active aid of our representative to that government and through the intimidation caused by the presence of an armed naval force of the United States, which was landed for that purpose at the instance of our minister," Cleveland told Congress in his annual message in December. "Upon the facts developed it seemed to me the only honorable course for our government to pursue was to undo the wrong that had been done by those representing us and to restore as far as practicable the status existing at the time of our forcible intervention." In order to restore the former government of the islands, the president repudiated the annexation treaty, withdrawing it from Senate consideration, and refused to annex Hawaii in any way.[18]

The Cleveland administration, however, was not able to restore Queen Liliuokalani to her throne. She vowed, upon return, to behead the rebels and seize their property. Cleveland worried about their fate and sought assurances from both sides that there would be no violence, even asking the queen to issue a general amnesty, but he was unable to get satisfactory answers. The new Democratic Congress bounced around solutions for months but remained largely indecisive, as was the president. Finally, Congress decided that the best option would be to simply recognize the provisional government that had been established after the coup, and its new president, Sanford Dole. Cleveland really had no other option but to go along. This sordid affair demonstrated the complications of becoming involved in the internal affairs of other nations.[19]

Despite the setback of failing to restore the status quo in Hawaii, Cleveland had fought back against the growing jingoist tide and won. His paramount objective was to keep out of the affair and allow Hawaiians to determine their own future. "The thing I care most about is the declaration that the *people* of the islands instead of the *provisional government* should determine the policy," he wrote Senator William Vilas. The people of Hawaii were the "source of power and control" over the islands. His policy received praise from members of both parties. Charles Francis Adams Jr., of the famed Adams family, wrote him that fall. "I remember no stand taken by a government so morally sound and dignified as that now taken by ... your administration," he said, a stance that would make American foreign policy stronger. "It is not easy to see how the United States can protest against the policy of force in [British] dealings with semi-civilized natives and races, if we ourselves are quite unable to resist the temptation to have an occasional hack at them on our own account."[20]

Harrison's attempt to annex Hawaii and Cleveland's defeat of it "constitute one of the most unjustly neglected episodes in American diplomatic history," writes Cleveland biographer Allan Nevins. But Hawaii would not long remain independent. When Republican William McKinley came to the White House in 1897, annexation proceeded with vigor. Upon assuming the presidency, he lost no time negotiating a new treaty of annexation, which was sent to the Senate that summer. But the Japanese protested, fearing annexation might jeopardize treaty rights for Japanese inhabitants in Hawaii. Japan was also suspicious of American motives with the annexation of territory in the Asian sphere of influence rightfully reserved for Asians. The Japanese government in Tokyo, however, was busy with its own expansion—defeating China in 1895, eventually annexing Korea in 1910, possessing Taiwan, and eyeing Manchuria. But Hawaii was also on their radar.[21]

But Japan would come up short. The annexation treaty lagged in the Senate, with stiff opposition from anti-imperialists in and out of Congress. But in August 1898, after the Spanish-American War, Hawaii was finally annexed when it became clear to a majority in Congress that the islands were of vital importance to the United States. Americans also used fear to persuade native Hawaiians of the need for annexation. They were told the Japanese were determined to seize the islands and completely destroy Hawaiian culture, something they did after occupying any new land. To overcome anti-imperialist opposition, particularly in the Senate, Congress used a joint resolution, the same process used to annex Texas in 1845, and not a treaty, which would have taken a two-thirds majority. "Hawaii is ours," wrote ex-President Cleveland to his former Secretary of State Richard Olney upon hearing the news. "As I look back upon the first steps in this miserable business, I am ashamed of the whole affair." Though he was unable to keep the islands permanently sovereign, many native Hawaiians still honor Cleveland for his efforts to protect their native government.[22]

LATIN AMERICA

The aggressive, imperialist impulses of the Harrison administration, along with the president's overzealous Secretary of State, made most of Latin America nervous about its future. In 1893, Latin Americans breathed a collective sigh of relief and welcomed Cleveland back to the White House, as the leaders of those nations saw him as an anti-imperialist who would protect the peace and security of the entire Western Hemisphere.[23]

And in Latin America, like Hawaii, President Cleveland faced another revolution, this one on the Spanish-controlled island of Cuba. Spain had maintained control of Cuba since Christopher Columbus, but by the late nineteenth century much of the Cuban population was unhappy with

Spanish rule and revolutionary disturbances broke out in the 1870s. The United States had been occupied with internal problems during those years but by the 1890s, with the renewed interest in foreign affairs, specifically sought the construction of a canal across the Isthmus of Panama or Nicaragua. Cuba was close to the proposed canal and would be vital to its protection, so this gave the United States more reason to be concerned with internal stability there, which became more disturbing in the 1890s when another revolution broke out on the island.

Scholars generally cite two causes for the Cuban Revolution in the 1890s. An obvious reason would be the incompetent and sometimes brutal rule of the Spaniards. But a second and more important factor concerned an economic crisis in Cuba caused in part by a shift in US tariff policy, namely the adoption of the 1894 Wilson-Gorman tariff. Eighty percent of the economy of Cuba was based on sugar, and under the 1890 McKinley tariff, Cuban sugar entered the US market duty free. But the 1894 tariff placed high duties on Cuban sugar, which helped bring economic collapse to the island.[24]

Against this backdrop, the Cubans rose up against Spanish rule in February 1895, an uprising that turned into a civil war with atrocities on both sides, as both combatants conducted themselves in a very uncivilized manner. Under the rule of Spanish governor-general Valeriano Weyler, Cubans in rural areas were garrisoned in concentration camps guarded by Spanish troops, one of the first uses in history. Anyone outside the camps would be considered a rebel and could be shot on sight. For their part, the Cubans conducted a "scorched-earth" policy by burning sugar plantations and government buildings. Since US business controlled most Cuban sugar, the Cuban revolutionaries wanted the business interest to pressure the US government to intervene.[25]

And the business influence was considerable. With investments totaling $50 million, Americans had great wealth invested in the island, with trade between Cuba and the United States amounting to nearly $100 million in 1894, quite a lucrative deal that no one wanted to see lost. But President Cleveland had no desire to intervene in Cuba on the behalf of the insurgents. The United States "is in truth the most pacific of powers and desires nothing so much as to live in amity with all the world. Its own ample and diversified domains satisfy all possible longings for territory, preclude all dreams of conquest, and prevent any casting of covetous eyes upon neighboring regions, however attractive," he wrote in an annual message to Congress.[26]

But the jingoistic attitude toward Cuba was at a fever pitch. President Cleveland referred to it as an "epidemic of insanity." Congressional leaders traveled to Woodley, Cleveland's private residence outside Washington, in order to persuade him to change his opinion, which was a near impossibility once he made his mind up, and in regard to Cuba, he had. With the president unwilling to budge, Republicans in Congress threatened to declare war on Cuba without him, for conditions there were "intolerable," they said. Cleveland replied, "There shall be no war with Spain over Cuba as long as I am president." If Congress declared war, he would not, as commander-in-chief, mobilize the army. Why fight, he asked, when the US government could buy the island for $150 million if desired? A war would probably cost more lives and treasure than anyone realized, as well as burden the taxpayers with another long list of pensioners, all of it completely unnecessary, he felt. Instead of war, Cleveland signed two neutrality proclamations in regard to Cuba in the summer of 1895 and again in 1896, prohibiting Americans from becoming involved with the internal disturbances on the island. The United States also made two attempts to mediate the dispute in 1896 and 1897, to no avail. Cleveland also asked the Spanish to institute political reforms but was rebuffed.[27]

Jingoists did not like Cleveland's non-aggressive approach. One opposition imperialist in particular was Theodore Roosevelt, a self-described "Cuba Libre man" who wanted the president to "interfere" and send the "fleet promptly to Havana." To Teddy, war was a virtuous benefit and should be used as an instrument of national policy. As assistant secretary of the navy under McKinley in 1897, Roosevelt addressed the Naval War College with this pronouncement: "All the great masterful races have been fighting races, and the minute that a race loses the hard fighting virtues, then, no matter what else it may retain, no matter how skilled in commerce and finance, in science or art, it has lost its proud right to stand as the equal of the best." He had no patience for anyone who sought a softer approach.[28]

But Cleveland believed that war with Spain, in addition to costs, would destabilize Cuba. How would the island fare if, all of a sudden, it fell into the hands of insurgent rebels not accustomed to governing themselves? If chaos reigned, then it might invite European intervention, a not uncommon occurrence, particularly in matters of debt default. Yet Cleveland was every bit the nineteenth-century man on matters of race, and he did not believe the Cubans capable of self-government. Imperialists like TR believed much the same thing, but they had an alternate plan. Though the Cubans might nominally be in charge after US intervention and removal of Spain, the Americans would administer the country in actuality. To Cleveland, this was just as unacceptable.

On March 4, 1897, William McKinley, who won the presidency the previous November over William Jennings Bryan, was sworn in as Cleveland's successor and would have Cuba as much on his mind as he did Hawaii. The evening before the inauguration, Cleveland hosted a dinner for him at the White House, where he told the president-elect that any conflict with Spain over Cuba, in his opinion, could be a "catastrophe." McKinley felt the same way, or at least that's what he told Cleveland, but the incoming commander-in-chief was much more sympathetic to the notion of intervention on behalf of Cuban rebels than his predecessor.[29]

When the tide of war came in 1898, McKinley did not have the strength to stop it even if he had wanted to, which he did not. The "splendid little war" was over in no time, allowing the United States to establish a protectorate over Cuba and then grab Guam, Puerto Rico, and, most importantly, the Philippines, which further fueled Japanese suspicion. Though not viewed as a progressive like his successor Theodore Roosevelt, McKinley did inaugurate the era of American imperialism, which can be seen as the application of progressivism abroad. Under McKinley, America bit into the "forbidden fruit of imperialism" for the first time, wrote Pat Buchanan, "leading to America's involvement in all the great wars of the twentieth century."[30]

UPHOLDING THE MONROE DOCTRINE

Many jingoists took Cleveland's non-interventionist policies for passivism, or in Theodore Roosevelt's opinion, outright cowardice. Cleveland did believe in a more aggressive foreign policy, if the case called for it, as it did when he sent warships to China and Korea to protect American missionaries, but never for imperialistic reasons. He believed strongly in the principle of self-determination of peoples, and in the Monroe Doctrine as an instrument to safeguard the country and the American sphere of influence, having demonstrated his attachment to it with his opposition to the British loan offer to Hawaii. He did not believe the doctrine should be used for aggressive purposes, such as acquiring more territory, but only to protect American rights. If one could sum up Cleveland's foreign policy in a short, simple phrase, it would be "maintain the status quo" if at all possible. He did not side with "rebels" in Hawaii or in Cuba, although he sympathized with them, for he believed that to intervene would be to make the current situation much worse. He understood better than the imperialists that intervening militarily in the internal affairs of another nation could be a chaotic and bloody proposition, as the United States found out in the Philippines in 1898, where an eventual five-year insurgency would claim 4,000 American lives, and with an all-too-familiar situation in Iraq in the first decade of the 2000s, where thousands more were sacrificed.

There were methods other than intervention that could be employed when trouble arose with foreign nations. In a messy internal situation in Brazil, where the government was under siege in what had become a civil war between "monarchists" and "republicans," Cleveland again came to the rescue of the government in power, sending a naval fleet of five ships to the coast to break a rebel blockade. The aggressive show of force, along with a private flotilla of armed merchant and passenger ships under Charles Flint, helped keep the republican government of Brazil intact. The grateful Brazilians constructed a monument to honor James Monroe and his famous doctrine, which Cleveland invoked so often in Latin America.[31]

But before his second term was up, he faced a much more serious potential threat to the hemisphere when he tangled with the British in a boundary dispute involving Venezuela. What might have been regarded as a minor disagreement involved the location of the western boundary of British Guiana, which bordered Venezuela, in an area between the Orinoco and Essiquibo rivers, encompassing a significant and lucrative chunk of Venezuelan territory. Britain had taken over the Guiana territory from the Dutch in 1814, and the exact boundary line had never been firmly established. The problem festered for years. Both sides thought the matter more than a minor one and suspended diplomatic relations in 1887. Venezuela, knowing President Cleveland's regard for Latin America, asked for Washington's assistance on several occasions, appeals for help that were "incessantly ringing in our ears," Cleveland wrote.[32]

American citizens, as well as members of Congress, were becoming increasingly alarmed by European incursions in the Western Hemisphere, particularly by the British. Cleveland determined not to allow any further encroachment by European powers into the Americas. He believed the British taking even an inch of Venezuelan territory would be a violation of the Monroe Doctrine. To solve the dispute, the president sought international arbitration as the preferred method for bringing the issue to a successful conclusion. Secretary of State Richard Olney sent a non-threatening note to the British government inviting them to arbitration. But London simply ignored the inquiry.

The arrogance of the British angered Cleveland, who then ordered Olney to send a strongly worded message to get their attention. The president specified that he wanted to use the Monroe Doctrine, though Olney was a bit skeptical at first. In what became known as the Olney Corollary to the Monroe Doctrine, the secretary of state boasted, "The United States is practically sovereign on this continent, and its fiat is law upon the subjects to which it confines its interposition," while "its infinite resources combined with its isolated position render it master of the situation and practically invulnerable as against any or all other powers." Not exactly a delicate diplomatic message, but it had Cleveland's full support.[33]

The British Prime Minister, Lord Salisbury, waited four months before responding to Olney's jab with a shot of his own, denying that the United States had any power and authority to command Britain in the Western Hemisphere. Cleveland responded with a strong message of his own on December 17, 1895. Britain had taken possession of territory of a neighboring republic "against its will and in derogation of its rights," he told Congress, making it likely that Britain will "attempt to extend its system of government to that portion of this continent which it has thus taken." This was precisely why Monroe issued his doctrine in the first place, he reminded the members. The British government might deny that the Monroe Doctrine had any authority in the matter, but to Cleveland that counted little. He vowed to use it to prevent what he perceived as an injustice toward Venezuela. The tough words caused many Americans to conclude that war was on the horizon. But that was never Cleveland's intention. Forcing Britain to arbitration was. As Secretary of the Navy Hilary A. Herbert, who hailed from Alabama and served during the second administration, wrote, Cleveland "meant peace not war," for the

White House knew that Britain was "not ready to go to war with us for the protection of unscrupulous British adventurers who were overrunning Venezuelan frontiers."[34]

In the end of a very long and complicated affair, the British backed down, recognizing, in principle at least, the Monroe Doctrine. A commission was then set up to determine the boundary issue. To their credit, Cleveland and Olney did not seek to embarrass the British but allowed them to withdraw gracefully. For their part, the British did have more pressing concerns elsewhere and probably did not want to risk war with the United States over a small plot of jungle in the wilds of the Amazon.[35]

Historians, though, have accused Cleveland of "wagging the dog" in his intervention in Venezuela in order to distract the American people from the ongoing economic woes with the Panic of 1893. These opinions about Cleveland do not reflect fresh thinking and were regurgitated from what opposition politicians were saying at the time. Regardless of their origin, the theory is patently absurd. The incident with Britain did not become tense until the latter part of 1895, the last half of his second term when the economy was on the rebound. Why would Cleveland have waited until then to "wag the dog?" The economy was in much worse shape in 1893 and 1894, and the president had a huge opportunity in Hawaii, as well as in Cuba, to distract attention but he did not. Furthermore, an international incident with the British Empire, which many thought would lead to war, would only panic markets further, not cause an economic rally.

Grover Cleveland did not believe in such unscrupulous tactics; he stuck to his principles instead. He did what he believed was right, regardless of the consequences. Diplomatic historian Thomas A. Bailey, who does not hold Cleveland in high regard, nevertheless praised one result of the Venezuelan crisis. The "United States, having stared down the British Lion, emerged with enhanced standing among the powers of the world."[36]

Though he forced Lord Salisbury to back down, even as the Prime Minister tried to lecture him as a parent would a child, Cleveland demonstrated his toughness, and for that the British came to respect him. When Cleveland died in 1908, the *Morning Post* of London wrote that he "was one of the great men of his time. He had Bismarck's strength and Bismarck's breadth of views and more than Bismarck's honesty. As president he did not lift a finger for the Democratic Party but merely served the United States. He was the strongest man who has lived in the White House since the death of Washington."[37]

Some of America's foremost foreign policy scholars agree. President Cleveland, writes George Herring, "was not afraid to make tough foreign policy decisions. He displayed on occasion an admirable tendency to do the right thing for the right reason, injecting an element of morality into an area of endeavor and political climate where it was normally absent." For Cleveland believed, as did John Quincy Adams, that America "goes not abroad in search of monsters to destroy. She is the well-wisher to the freedom and independence of all. She is the champion and vindicator only of her own." Cleveland believed in the right of self-determination, beautifully enunciated by Jefferson in the Declaration of Independence, a cherished right that he thought should apply to all the peoples in the world.[38]

Endnotes

1   Cleveland, First Annual Message to Congress, December 4, 1893, Richardson, ed., *Messages and Papers*, XII, 5866–92.

2   This theory has been put forward by William E. Leuchtenburg, "Progressivism and Imperialism: The Progressive Movement and American Foreign Policy, 1898–1916," *Mississippi Valley Historical Review* (December 1952), 483–504.

3   Mark D. Hirsch, *William C. Whitney: Modern Warwick* (New York: Archon Books, 1948), 297-302, 335–6; Graff, 77.

4   Robert I. Rotberg, *The Founder: Cecil Rhodes and the Pursuit of Power* (New York: Oxford University Press, 1988), 100; Matthew Sweet, "Cecil Rhodes: A Bad Man in Africa," *The Independent*, March 16, 2002, http://www.independent.co.uk/news/world/africa/story.jsp?story=274990.

5   Rudyard Kipling, "The White Man's Burden," 1899, http://www.poetryloverspage.com/poets/kipling/white_mans_burden.html.

6   George C. Herring, *From Colony To Superpower: US Foreign Relations Since 1776* (Oxford: Oxford University Press, 2008), 299; John James Ingalls, *A Collection of the Writings of John James Ingalls: Essays, Addresses, and Orations* (Kansas City, MO: Hudson-Kimberly Publishing Co., 1902), 507.

7   E. L. Godkin to Charles Eliot Norton, December 29, 1895, *The Gilded Age Letters of E. L. Godkin*, edited by William M. Armstrong (Albany, NY: State University of New York Press, 1974), 475.

8   Herring, 303; Warren Zimmerman, *First Great Triumph: How Five Americans Made Their Country a World Power* (New York: Farrar, Straus and Giroux, 2004), 87–95.

9   Nevins, *Cleveland*, 551.

10   *Ibid.*

11   Robert Kagan, *Dangerous Nation: America's Place in the World from Its Earliest Days to the Dawn of the Twentieth Century* (New York: Alfred A. Knopf, 2006), 324–5.

12   *Ibid.*; Nevins, *Cleveland*, 550.

13   Nevins, *Cleveland*, 550.

14 *Ibid.*, 325; Herring, 296.

15 Stephen Kinzer, *Overthrow: America's Century of Regime Change from Hawaii to Iraq* (New York: Times Books, 2006), 9; Tom Coffman, *The Island Edge of America: A Political History of Hawaii* (Honolulu: University of Hawaii Press, 2003), 9–10.

16 Nevins, *Cleveland*, 551; Kagan, 326; Herring, 296–7.

17 Cleveland, First Annual Message to Congress (Second Term), December 4, 1893, Richardson, ed., *Messages and Papers*, XII, 5866–92; Nevins, *Cleveland*, 554.

18 Cleveland, First Annual Message to Congress (Second Term), December 4, 1893, Richardson, ed., *Messages and Papers*, XII, 5866–92.

19 Herring, 306.

20 Cleveland to Senator William F. Vilas, May 29, 1894, and Charles Francis Adams, Jr., to Cleveland, November 18, 1893, Nevins, *Letters*, 339, 353.

21 Coffman, 19–20.

22 Nevins, *Cleveland*, 549; Cleveland to Olney, July 8, 1898, Nevins, *Letters*, 502.

23 Nevins, *Cleveland*, 549–50.

24 Pat Buchanan, *The Great Betrayal: How American Sovereignty and Social Justice Are Being Sacrificed to the Gods of the Global Economy* (New York: Little, Brown, 1998), 216–7.

25 Kagan, 376.

26 Kagan, 376; Herring, 310; Cleveland, Fourth Annual Message (Second Term), December 7, 1896, Richardson, ed., *Messages and Papers*, XIII, 6146–77.

27 Richard Watson Gilder to H. G., September 1896, *Letters*, 298-299; A. B. Farquhar, *The First Million the Hardest: An Autobiography* (New York: Doubleday, 1922), 270–71; Cleveland, Proclamation 377, June 12, 1895 and Proclamation 387, July 27, 1896, Richardson, ed., *Messages and Papers*, XIII, 6023-4 and 6126-7.

28 Jim Powell, *Bully Boy: The Truth About Theodore Roosevelt's Legacy* (New York: Crown Forum, 2006), 36.

29 Parker, *Recollections*, 249.

30 Pat Buchanan, *A Republic, Not an Empire: Reclaiming America's Destiny* (Washington DC: Regnery Publishing, Inc., 1999), 141.

31 Herring, 306; Kagan, 368.

32 Nevins, *Cleveland,* 630; Grover Cleveland, *Presidential Problems* (New York: The Century Company, 1904), 247.

33 Henry James, *Richard Olney and His Public Service* (Boston: Houghton Mifflin, 1923), 109.

34 Cleveland, Special Message on Venezuela, December 17, 1895, Richardson, ed., *Messages and Papers,* XIII, 6087–90; Herbert, "Grover Cleveland and His Cabinet At Work," *Century Magazine,* March 1913, 742.

35 Gerald G. Eggert, *Richard Olney: Evolution of a Statesman* (University Park, PA: Penn State University Press, 1974), 232–3.

36 Thomas A. Bailey, *Presidential Greatness: The Image and the Man from George Washington to the Present* (New York: Appleton-Century, 1966), 300.

37 *The New York Times,* June 25, 1908.

38 Herring, 278; John Quincy Adams, Address of July 4, 1821, in Walter LaFeber, ed., *John Quincy Adams and American Continental Empire: Letters, Papers and Speeches* (Chicago: Quadrangle Books, 1965), 45.

Chapter 6

PARTY DESTROYER OR DEFENDER OF PRINCIPLE?

"I never submitted the whole system of my opinions to the creed of any party of men whatever ... where I was capable of thinking for myself. Such an addiction is the last degradation of a free and moral agent. If I could not go to heaven but with a party, I would not go there at all."

—Thomas Jefferson to Francis Hopkinson,
March 13, 1789

"Let me rise or fall, I am going to work for the interests of the people of the state, regardless of party or anything else."

—Grover Cleveland, in the *Buffalo Daily Courier,*
August 10, 1884

Grover Cleveland always stood on principle, no matter the consequences or the criticism. For that reason, he was widely admired and much sought after for public office. "Cleveland was a party man without answering to the ordinary conception of a politician," wrote Elihu Root, Secretary of State under Theodore Roosevelt. "He had strong common sense, simplicity, and directness without subtlety, instinctive and immovable integrity, perfect courage, a kindly nature with great capacity for friendship, and with great capacity also for wrath, which made him a dangerous man to trifle with."[1]

DEFENDER OF JEFFERSONIAN PRINCIPLES

In 1882, the New York Democratic Party found itself in the political wilderness. A state party leader, Edgar K. Apgar, wrote to Cleveland, then the mayor of Buffalo, to see if he would consider serving as governor. The Democratic Party, he wrote, "has so often, in recent years, abandoned its principles and made dishonest alliances for the sake of temporary success, which even in most cases it has failed to secure," and has "largely lost the confidence of the people." The party "has fallen, in so many instances, into bad hands," causing many to distrust "our promises of reform." The party had only itself to blame, in Apgar's eyes:

> If we had stood faithfully by Jeffersonian principles; if we had exercised all the power of legitimate party discipline to destroy corruption and demagoguism in our own ranks; if we had been content to deserve success and to wait for it, we would, in my judgment, have been for many years firmly entrenched in power in the State and nation. The weakness of our present position, in which we seem to depend more upon Republican dissensions and decay than upon any strength of our own, is, I think, much more due to our failures in the directions I have indicated than it is to any personal or factional quarrels which have existed among us.[2]

The solution was simple: find a steadfast man of Jeffersonian principles to head the New York Democratic ticket in 1882 and maybe the national ticket in 1884. They found that man in Grover Cleveland of Buffalo, New York.

Cleveland always held the people in the highest regard, much higher than the party itself. After winning the governorship, Cleveland told a reporter from the *Buffalo Daily Courier*, "Let me rise or fall, I am going to work for the interests of the people of the state, regardless of party or anything else." When he ran for president in 1884, he chose as his campaign slogan "A Public Office is a Public Trust," a motto that perfectly captured his personal principles, of which he wrote a friend, "Above all, let us constantly be reminded that the good of the people and the protection of their interests is the supreme duty of all public officers." Politicians often dodge issues, water-down past records and statements, and outright lie about their intentions, but Cleveland remained true to what he believed. "I am a Democrat attached to the principles of the party; and if elected, I desire to remain true to that organization," he wrote to a fellow Jeffersonian. He believed in the existence of the party system, but to be used as a vehicle to espouse "well-defined and understood party principles," rather than for "the hope of personal reward and advantage" for its members. The Democratic Party should rest on doing what's best for "the welfare of the country and the prosperity of our people." Throughout his great public career, he desired above all "that the *party* shall demonstrate its usefulness and fitness to hold the government."[3]

When he won the nomination for president in 1884, he wrote an official letter of acceptance to the party's national committee. "We proudly call ours a government by the people," he told Democratic leaders. "It is not such when a class is tolerated which arrogates to itself the management of public affairs, seeking to control the people, instead of representing them. Parties are the necessary outgrowths of our institutions; but a government is not by the people when one party fastens its control upon the country and perpetuates its power by cajoling and betraying the people instead of serving them. A government is not by the people when a result which should represent the intelligent will of free and thinking men is or can be determined by the shameless corruption of their suffrages." He intended to bring about a "full realization of a government by the people."[4]

After he won his first White House race, he well knew the difficult task ahead. "I look upon the four years next to come as a dreadful self-inflicted penance for the good of my country," he wrote his best friend, Wilson S. Bissell, in Buffalo. "I can see no pleasure in it and no satisfaction, only a hope that I may be of service to my people." He was ready to do his duty for those who elected him, tackling the major issues that would confront him, some old, some new – the never-ending battle between protectionists and free traders; emerging conflicts between labor and management; continuing arguments over monetary policy between advocates of the gold standard and those who favored an inflationary currency; and fights between civil service reformers and hardline machine politicians. According to Alyn Brodsky, Cleveland was prepared "to sacrifice his influence – if need be, his presidency – in pursuit of what he believed was best for the nation."[5]

Defeated for a second presidential term in 1888, Cleveland retired and had no thought of returning to public life. The only living Democratic president, though, was a hot commodity, and party members across the country sought his help. But Cleveland kept his principles even when out of office. He did not think it proper for ex-presidents to be out campaigning, a situation that was "against the ideas and traditions of our people." He received an invitation to speak on behalf of the party in Ohio, a politically important state for the midterm elections in 1890. The big issue that year, and throughout the rest of the decade, was the nation's currency – whether to maintain the gold standard or allow the free coinage of silver. Ohio had gone the way of silver and inserted a free silver plank into its platform. It was a growing movement within the party that greatly concerned Cleveland. He steadfastly advocated the gold standard throughout his life, so campaigning for a "Silver Democrat" party would compromise his principles. He would never espouse free silver simply to help someone get elected. That was out of the question. Silverites, he wrote a political friend in Ohio, would most likely "resent the importation of a speaker who has put himself on record as unequivocally as I have in opposition ... to free, unlimited, and independent silver coinage." And though many Democrats would accuse him of being "selfish," he would never compromise his principles to win an election.[6]

Members of both parties saw these strong traits in him. "In long-range perspective Grover Cleveland stands out as one of the great figures of our political history," wrote his personal secretary, Robert Lincoln O'Brien. "It was not only his eight years of conscientious service as president but also the tenacity with which he stuck to his principles and the vigor with which he fought for them that made him preeminent." Republican Senator Shelby Cullom of Illinois greatly admired him for his strength in the face of party pressure. "As chief executive, Cleveland was strong-minded and forceful and adhered to his views on public questions with a remarkable degree of tenacity, utterly regardless of his party," he wrote in his memoirs. For Ambassador Andrew Dickson White, "Cleveland ... seemed utterly incapable of making any bid for mob support; there had appeared not the slightest germ of demagoguism in him; he had refused to be a mere partisan tool and had steadily stood for the best ideals of government."[7]

WATCHDOG OF THE TREASURY

One principle he would stand firm on was the public purse. Throughout his public life, Cleveland viciously guarded the public treasury, even in times of economic hardship for the nation, using what one cabinet officer termed "his sledgehammer veto" to keep Congress in line. Even in his day, progressives in Congress, the state legislatures, and city councils could not quell the urge to tax and spend, but Cleveland believed it the job of the executive to quash their overzealous desires. He didn't just scrutinize and single out special appropriations like earmarks, pensions for veterans, or seed to farmers; he examined every spending bill that crossed his desk and killed every one he believed an unauthorized assault on the treasury, regardless of what group desired it.[8]

"Economy in public expenditure," he repeatedly reminded Congress, "is a duty that can not innocently be neglected by those entrusted with the control of money drawn from the people for public uses." To accomplish economy in public spending, he employed a chief executive's most powerful weapon: the veto. Cleveland possessed a very strong Jacksonian concept of the veto power, even stronger than Old Hickory himself. The nation's first six presidents vetoed only legislation they believed to be in violation of the Constitution, but President Jackson, the nation's seventh chief executive, rejected any bill he disagreed with ideologically, whether constitutional or not, ushering in an era of the "unlimited veto." Presidents Washington through John Quincy Adams cancelled ten bills; Jackson vetoed twelve. But Cleveland took Jackson's policy to a whole new level, killing 414 congressional acts in his first presidential term alone. Whereas Jackson used the veto to strengthen the presidency, as well as his own position over Congress, Cleveland used it as a whip to discipline the people's representatives and protect taxpayers from legislative extravagance.[9]

Aside from the presidency, Cleveland was just as tough in his local and state offices. As mayor of Buffalo and governor of New York, he cancelled many spending bills that legislators tried to slip by him in order to benefit and reward favored constituents. As mayor of Buffalo, Cleveland had no tolerance or patience when it came to wasteful and unnecessary spending, particularly appropriations that violated the state constitution. On one occasion, he vetoed two resolutions that illegally provided funds for dubious purposes. The first directed $500 to the Fireman's Benevolent Association, which to some would be a fitting gesture, but Cleveland pointed out the specific clause in the state's constitution that prohibited cities and counties from spending money on such causes. The second provided another $500 to the decorating committee of the Grand Army of the Republic to be spent celebrating Decoration Day, what we now call Memorial Day. Though he deemed the intent "a most worthy one," the bill violated the same provision of the state constitution, as well as the city's charter. Any money given to causes such as these, he wrote in his veto message, "should be a free gift of the citizens and taxpayers, and should not be extorted from them by taxation. This is so, because the purpose for which this money is asked does not involve their protection or interest as members of the community." An appropriation to such an endeavor would, in his mind, be "oppressive and unjust." The mayor then led by example in making a personal donation of $50 to the committee. The *Buffalo Daily Courier* praised his vetoes, calling his arguments "unanswerable."[10]

Mayor Cleveland also cancelled a supplemental appropriation to award $800 to each of three German newspapers in Buffalo to print the city council's proceedings. The council, and not the mayor, had the authority to designate an official paper for the city government, and the politicians wanted to make sure that three German papers were included. These papers were very important within the large German community, particularly during campaign season. That being said, Cleveland, in his only annual message as mayor, reminded the council that "work of this description, like all others, should be done where it can be done the cheapest." Such an endeavor "is not accomplished when it is bestowed as a professional reward for party service or an item of political patronage."[11]

Ignoring the mayor's words, the council appropriated money to circulate their proceedings in the city's official paper but also passed a supplemental appropriation to allocate funds to the German papers. Cleveland quickly vetoed the supplemental bill. He surmised that the German papers would publish a synopsis of the proceedings on their own, in order to be of benefit to their readers. The "effect of the resolution is to give these newspapers $800 each for doing no more than they will in a sense be obliged to do without it." That did not stop the council, however.

The members were determined to reward these German publications with tax dollars, passing a new appropriation to publish tax sale notices in all three German newspapers for $150 each. Cleveland again rejected the resolution. The council finally gave up.[12]

The "Veto Mayor," as he was dubbed, tackled many minor projects that were rife with corruption. He killed a warrant to pay the city comptroller an extra $27 for nine nights of overtime work because the employee was already on the payroll drawing an annual salary. He also stopped payments to city workers who wanted to use city horses and wagons for private livery services, blocked the newly created job of morgue keeper, and ended the funding of unnecessary sidewalks. He then reformed the contract procedure to ensure competitive bidding for city projects, helping end many scams.[13]

His passion for saving taxpayer funds did not change when he became governor the following year. Soon after entering his duties in Albany, Cleveland quickly emerged as the "Veto Governor," swiftly killing eight bills within his first month in office, mainly issues relating to local governments. He denied Montgomery County the right to borrow money because the repayment plan involved unfair double taxation, stopped several proposals by various cities to make illegal revisions to their charters, including Buffalo and Elmira, the hometown of his Lt. Governor, and vetoed a proposal that would have allowed Chautauqua County to appropriate funds for a monument to its fallen soldiers, a similar action he had taken as mayor. He did not dislike such enterprises but felt such projects should be funded only by private donations and not taxpayer dollars. When a Catholic group sought state funds to establish an orphanage in New York City, he vetoed the measure on constitutional grounds.[14]

Even hometown friends, who might have thought their association with him would gain special favors, quickly found they were sadly mistaken. He vetoed a bill to reorganize the fire department in Buffalo, a scheme he believed was rife with corruption. His action led the *Albany Evening Journal* to call the veto "strong and wise." He also killed a measure that would have allowed his boyhood home of Fayetteville to borrow money to buy a fire engine. And to keep the government out of the banking business, Cleveland vetoed a measure that would authorize the state comptroller to lessen the liabilities of the First National Bank of Buffalo after it failed, a blow to the banking industry.[15]

No one received free rides on the back of taxpayers under Governor Grover Cleveland. Public money would be used for the basic functions of government and nothing more. Not even the state's military veterans would gain from the public trough. The legislature approved a bill to provide relief to the surviving members of the First Regiment of New York Volunteers, a unit that served in the Mexican War in the 1840s. The act would provide pensions of $12 a month for the next two years, at a total cost to taxpayers of $14,976. In shades of his presidency, Governor Cleveland vetoed the pension measure as unnecessary, since the state had already appropriated $60,000 for just such a purpose in preceding years and "further relief ought not be insisted on." It was, he told the legislature, a "question of principle ... that justice to the taxpayer should replace the generosity of the State." Even though his party controlled the legislature, Cleveland vetoed forty-four bills during his first session and a total of two hundred during his two years as governor.[16]

When he first entered the White House in 1885, the public debt was $1.5 billion, with expenditures of only $260 million. Revenue, however, totaled $323 million, a surplus of $63 million. When he lost his bid for reelection in 1888, his frugal policies had swelled the surplus to $111 million, while the national debt had been cut to $1.2 billion. With such high amounts of revenue and surpluses, Cleveland wanted to give it back to the taxpayers but failed twice to enact a cut in tariffs and other taxes. The high rates had generated the surplus, which was simply over-taxation he felt, and should be given back to the people. The surplus money is "hoarded in the Treasury when it should be in their hands," he told Congress, "or we should be drawn into wasteful public extravagance, with all the corrupting national demoralization which follows in its train." He knew if the surplus remained in the treasury, Congress would surely spend it.[17]

In 1896, the final year of his second term in the White House, the Republicans, who took control of Congress during the 1894 midterms, tried again to spend more money, even though the economy, then suffering the ravages of the Panic of 1893, was still not in good shape in terms of unemployment. But to help the situation, they sent Cleveland a bill for river and harbor construction, the major infrastructure spending at that time, what amounted to a Keynesian-style stimulus that was full of earmarked projects across the country. Even though he had only a short time left in office, Cleveland would not support it. "There are 417 items of appropriation contained in this bill," the president noted, "and every part of the country is represented in the distribution of its favors." Unsurprisingly, he vetoed the bill. "In view of the obligation imposed upon me by the Constitution, it seems to me quite clear that I only discharge a duty to our people when I interpose my disapproval of the legislation proposed," he wrote Congress in his veto message. "Many of the objects for which it appropriates public money are not related to the public welfare, and many of them are palpably for the benefit of limited localities or in aid of individual interests." To sign such a spending bill would be to violate fundamental principles. "Economy and the exaction of clear justification for the appropriation of public moneys by the servants of the people are not only virtues but solemn obligations." From his first days as a sheriff and small-town mayor until his last day as president, Grover Cleveland never lost one ounce of his enthusiasm for the American taxpayer.[18]

His zealous regard for public money was almost obsessive. A popular story told at the time revealed his constant concern for public money and congressional attempts to steal it. Resting at his presidential retreat, Oak View, during a weekend, his frightened wife, Frances, shook Grover awake in the dead of night, crying out, "Wake up! There are burglars in the house!" A groggy president replied, "No, no, my dear. In the Senate maybe, but not in the House." Whether the story is true or not makes little difference. His affection for taxpayers was well known and his duty to protect them from fraud and theft would never wane during his political career.[19]

UPHOLDING THE CONSTITUTION

There's little doubt that the Constitution has lost much of its relevance over time. To some it has become what Alexander Hamilton always hoped it would be, "a frail and worthless fabric." This is particularly true since the Lincolnian revolution of 1861-1865 when the Constitution was not allowed to stand in the way of what the North wanted to do. All constitutional questions have been turned over to the Supreme Court in our time, though the Founders never had that intention in mind.

In earlier times, though, presidents believed they had as much right as Congress or the Supreme Court to rule on the constitutionality of laws. Thomas Jefferson was always skeptical about the right of the Supreme Court to exercise judicial review. "The question whether the judges are invested with exclusive authority to decide on the constitutionality of a law has been heretofore a subject of consideration with me in the exercise of official duties. Certainly there is not a word in the Constitution which has given that power to them more than to the Executive or Legislative branches." He believed the federal courts, operating under this extra-constitutional power, were establishing a judicial tyranny over the rest of the government. The Constitution, he wrote Abigail Adams, "meant that its coordinate branches should be checks on each other. But the opinion which gives to the judges the right to decide what laws are constitutional and what not, not only for themselves in their own sphere of action but for the Legislature and Executive also in their spheres, would make the Judiciary a despotic branch." President Jefferson and his majority party in Congress were so hostile to the federal judiciary that they used impeachment against out-of-control judges and enacted the Judiciary Act of 1802 that abolished sixteen judgeships, nearly half the entire court system.[20]

When early Jeffersonian presidents vetoed legislation, their messages contained constitutional arguments. In 1817, President James Madison, the Father of the Constitution, vetoed a public works bill, telling members of Congress that "such a power is not expressly given by the Constitution," nor could it "be deduced from any part of it without an inadmissible latitude of construction and reliance on insufficient precedents." His message continued: "The legislative powers vested in Congress are specified and enumerated in the eighth section of the first article of the Constitution, and it does not appear that the power proposed to be exercised by the bill is among the enumerated powers, or that it falls by any just interpretation with the power to make laws necessary and proper for carrying into execution those or other powers vested by the Constitution in the Government of the United States."[21]

Another good Jeffersonian president, and a great foe of centralization, was the much-maligned Franklin Pierce, who, as a "dough-face," a Northerner who held Southern principles, has drawn the ever-lasting, yet unjustified, ire of history. "The dangers of a concentration of all power in the general government of a confederacy so vast as ours are too obvious to be disregarded," he stated in his Inaugural Address on March 4, 1853. "You have a right, therefore, to expect your agents in every department to regard strictly the limits imposed upon them by the Constitution of the United States." This was not simply high-minded rhetoric. In 1854 Pierce vetoed a bill that would have provided government funds for the mentally insane, an early attempt at paternalism on the federal level. "I can not find any authority in the Constitution for ... public charity," he told Congress. "To do so would, in my judgment, be contrary to the letter and spirit of the Constitution and subversive of the whole theory upon which the Union of these states is founded."[22]

Grover Cleveland was one of the last American presidents to invoke the Constitution so forcefully. Unlike later presidents, he idolized the Jeffersonians and held the Constitution sacred, conveying that sentiment to the nation in his first Inaugural Address on March 4, 1885. In his speech from the East Portico of the US Capitol, Cleveland mentioned the Constitution eight times, elaborating at length on his strict Jeffersonian views. The Constitution "borne the hopes and the aspirations of a great people through prosperity and peace and through the shock of foreign conflicts and the perils of domestic strife and vicissitudes." It should be used "to promote the lasting welfare of the country and to secure the full measure of its priceless benefits to us and to those who will succeed to the blessings of our national life." In his capacity as president, Cleveland would "endeavor to be guided by a just and unstrained construction of the Constitution, a careful observance of the distinction between the powers granted to the federal government and those reserved to the States or to the people, and by a cautious appreciation of those functions which by the Constitution and laws have been especially assigned to the executive branch of the government."[23]

The Constitution and the government belonged to the people, he told his fellow citizens, and "the suffrage which executes the will of freemen is yours; the laws and the entire scheme of our civil rule, from the town meeting to the state capitals and the national capital, is yours." But with this comes great responsibility. "Your every voter ... exercises a public trust. Nor is this all. Every citizen owes to the country a vigilant watch and close scrutiny of its public servants and a fair and reasonable estimate of their fidelity and usefulness. This is the price of our liberty and the inspiration of our faith in the Republic." And in two terms as president,

Cleveland demonstrated his strong attachment to the Constitution on numerous occasions.

But as governor of New York, Cleveland also maintained his strong attachment to the US Constitution as well as that of his state. One of the most controversial acts to emerge from the legislature during Cleveland's governorship was a proposal known as the "Five-Cent Fare Bill." Jay Gould, a wealthy robber baron hated throughout New York, if not the country, owned an elevated train in the city. By charter, the rail line could charge ten cents for a ride, but lawmakers wanted the fare lowered to five cents. The legislature believed Gould made far too much in profit from the deal, money he subsequently hid from the taxman, they believed. The *New York Times* attacked the railway as one of the "greatest monopolies" and "one of the worst swindles" in New York State. Furthermore, the great majority of the people, particularly the poor, would benefit as a result of the government-imposed rate reduction. With the support of the major newspapers of the city and overwhelmingly passed by both houses, including the backing of Assembly Minority Leader Theodore Roosevelt, the bill was sent to Cleveland.[24]

On its face, the bill seemed like a good idea. Who would not support a law aimed at helping the poor as well as getting back at the hated Gould? Cleveland agreed with the bill's sentiments but in the end, after pondering it most of the night, vetoed the proposal. It was, he believed, an unconstitutional violation of the contract between Gould and the city, an agreement that allowed a charge of ten cents for a ticket. If Gould made lots of money from the deal, so be it. The contract could not be broken just because the government decided it no longer liked it. Though New York City scholars Edwin Burrows and Mike Wallace contend that fifty leading industrialists, such as J. P. Morgan and William H. Vanderbilt, heavily lobbied the governor to veto the "offending legislation," Cleveland acted out of a regard for the rule of law. "It seems to me that to arbitrarily reduce these fares," he wrote in his veto message, "at this time and under existing circumstances involves a breach of faith on the part of the state, and a betrayal of confidence that the state has invited."[25]

It was one of the toughest political decisions of his life, and he believed that it could very well wreck his blossoming public career. Journalist Andrew Dickson White commended him for the veto "in the face of the earnest advice of partisans who assured him that by doing so he would surely array against him the working classes of that city and virtually annihilate his political future. To this his answer was that whatever his sympathies for the working class might be, he could not, as an honest man, allow such a bill to pass, and come what might, he would not." After issuing the veto, Cleveland retired for the evening. That night he told a friend that he expected to awaken the next morning as the most unpopular man in the state of New York. But he did what he believed was right, with no regard for the political consequences.[26]

When he peered at the papers the next morning, however, he realized that his initial analysis had been somewhat mistaken. For the most part, he was being praised for his political courage, which made him feel "a good deal better." The *Albany Evening Journal*, while believing the people were being injured by Gould's rail service, called the veto "technically sound." The *New York Times* had supported the bill before its passage, editorializing that "the interests of the people cannot safely be subordinated to those of Jay Gould or any other capitalist rich and unscrupulous enough to purchase legislation." After the veto, the *Times* noted that the governor's action should not "cause much surprise." He acted to protect the "honor and good faith" of the state.[27]

The *New York Herald* praised his political courage in issuing the veto, stating that Cleveland "has done it boldly, with no attempt at disguise. We respect him for that. We expected as much from him." But the paper criticized the governor for casting "his lot on the side of the great corporations and corporate manipulators, and staked his chances for future political preferment on their favor." It is "quite touching to witness a hopeful presidential candidate choose his side in the coming struggle between them and the people for the control of the powers of government." This was among the first public mentions of Cleveland for higher office but an incorrect analysis. He was not on the side of the corporations, but that of the Constitution. He never would have acted based on politics.[28]

RESTORING PRESTIGE TO THE PRESIDENCY

When Thomas Jefferson entered the duties of his office in 1801, he had to contend with a burgeoning federal judiciary attempting to assert itself over the other two branches; when Cleveland came to the White House during the corrupt Gilded Age, the office of the presidency had lost a great deal of its prestige to Congress. Lincoln had been a powerful president, in truth much stronger than the Constitution allows, but Congress snatched that newfound power from his unfortunate and weakened successor, Andrew Johnson, and held it tight. According to Massachusetts Senator George F. Hoar, Congress was "unwilling to part with the prerogatives ... which had been wrenched from the feeble hand of Johnson." And after the wrenching, Congress held most of the political influence and believed itself best suited to run the nation, thereby placing the chief executive in a subservient role.[29]

Though it seems clear that the Framers intended for Congress to be the strongest of the three branches, it must remain within its constitutional bounds and cannot encroach on the powers of the other two. The historian Henry Adams, son of Charles Francis Adams, was highly critical of the relationship between Congress and the White House, as well as the performance of the government itself. Writing in 1870, before Cleveland came to office, Adams lamented that the "whole fabric of the government has been violently wrenched from its original balance," for "Congress has assumed authority which it was never intended to hold." The government "does not govern; Congress is inefficient, and shows itself more and more incompetent, as at presently constituted, to wield the enormous powers that are forced upon it, while the Executive, in its full enjoyment of theoretical independence, is practically deprived of its necessary strength by the jealousy of the Legislature."[30]

And the jealousy was strong. A president attempting to influence Congress, wrote Senator Hoar, would have been received "as a personal affront." When a member of Congress visited the White House, "it was to give, not to receive advice," he wrote. "Each of these stars kept his own orbit and shone in his sphere, within which he tolerated no intrusion from the president or from anybody else."[31]

Though several of his presidential predecessors tried and failed, it was Grover Cleveland who finally broke the congressional hold on power and restored the balance of authority, returning the presidency to a more dignified position in line with its constitutional duties. When Cleveland assumed office in 1885, the Senate attempted to dictate to him those officials he could and could not remove from office. They did this by invoking the Tenure of Office Act, the same tactic they used to impeach Andrew Johnson in 1868.

Congress passed the Tenure of Office Act in 1867, during the heated days of Reconstruction, in order to prevent President Johnson from removing any Senate-approved officials, mainly cabinet officers, without the consent of the Senate. As this law would give the Senate new authority over the executive branch, Johnson swiftly rejected it but Congress, overwhelmingly controlled by Radical Republicans, overrode the veto to make it the law of the land. In 1869 it was slightly diminished in scope, at the request of President Grant, but it remained strong nonetheless. Thus, the law had the effect of greatly weakening the presidency to the benefit of Congress, a deteriorating situation due in no small measure to the weak men who held the presidential office in those years.[32]

In the nineteenth century, before the vast majority of federal officeholders were chosen in the civil service system, the president appointed the entire bureaucracy, in most cases covering tens of thousands of positions. A new president from a different party held the power to remove everyone and replace them with members of his own party, a procedure that dated back to Andrew Jackson and came to be known as the "spoils system."

When Cleveland took office, after a quarter of a century of one-party rule, the federal bureaucracy was roughly 95 percent Republican and the GOP would have preferred it stay that way. Any removals seemed like a deep cut in the Republican flesh. After ten months in office, Cleveland had removed just 643 officials, mainly postmasters. Writing years later, Cleveland noted that he suspended these officials for "pernicious partisanship" and "official malfeasance." Postmasters were targeted because he learned that they were using their offices as headquarters for local Republican Party activities. Of these 643 officials, 500 of them protested directly to the Senate.[33]

But the epic showdown between the Senate and Cleveland stemmed from the President's removal, in July 1885, of the US Attorney for the Southern District of Alabama, George M. Duskin, a Republican. The president then named a Democrat, John D. Burnett, as Duskin's replacement. The Senate convened in December and, acting under the Tenure of Office Act, sought all documents concerning the removal of Duskin, but the president refused the request. Congress could request information on the appointment of nominees that required Senate approval, Cleveland informed them, but not for removals or suspensions.

The Senate Judiciary Committee then passed four resolutions that requested the information and formally censured Attorney General Augustus Garland "under whatever influence" he was operating under, an obvious reference to the president. Garland simply followed Cleveland's instructions in denying the Senate the materials it sought. In addition to the Department of Justice, Cleveland instructed all executive department officials to refuse to turn over materials related to any presidential suspensions and removals.[34]

Writing to Silas W. Burt, president of the New York Civil Service Reform Association, about the matter, the president ripped into "an unfriendly and political point-seeking Senate," whose members, at the time, were still appointed by the state legislatures, not elected by the people. He had withstood the "party every hour since I came into office" and refused "their demands in the full belief that I was doing something for the good of the Country and the purification of politics." Now, he continued, "I am to be treated like a thief and required to answer to the Senate for official acts the responsibility of which rests entirely upon me. Who made this arrogant body, far removed from the people, with granted privileges but no representative rights, the censor over the acts of a branch of the government elected by the people and answerable to them?" He hoped that by the time the dispute had ended, "the plain people of the land, who are substantially all the friends I have, shall understand the question."[35]

In direct response to the resolutions, the president sent a sharply worded special message to the Senate on March 1, 1886. "I believe the power to remove or suspend such officials is vested in the President alone by the Constitution," he wrote. "My oath to support and defend the Constitution, my duty to the people who have chosen me to execute the powers of their great office and not to relinquish them, and my duty to the Chief Magistracy, which I must preserve unimpaired in all its dignity and vigor, compel me to refuse compliance with these demands." Cleveland would not bow to the wishes of a "purgatorial Senate" whose only mission seemed to be partisan in nature, taken up to publicly shame the new president.[36]

But as the Senate soon found out, Grover Cleveland was no Andrew Johnson and the Senate eventually relented. Beaten in its fight, the Senate made no further requests of President Cleveland regarding the suspension and removal of officeholders. The president then convinced

Congress to repeal the Tenure of Office Act, for which it complied in March 1887, a bill Cleveland readily signed. The US Supreme Court eventually upheld Cleveland's position on the unconstitutionality of the Tenure of Office Act. As Philip Leigh has written, had the Tenure of Office Act prevailed, "the presidency could not have remained as an independent branch of government."[37]

His triumph over the upper chamber of Congress was complete, a great success that preserved the independence of the office, which had suffered greatly for decades. "He rescued the Presidency from two decades of Legislative encroachment on Executive power," wrote Dean Acheson. His victory, according to historian Richard E. Welch, Jr., was in the "perspective of a later day the most important reform achieved by Cleveland within the executive branch of government." The "entire episode marked a new phase in the history of the presidency," wrote Selig Adler. "The senatorial cabal which had dominated Grant, harassed Hayes, and caused so much trouble in the brief Garfield administration, had received a definite reverse. Cleveland's complete victory returned the office of President to a greater degree of executive independence and dominance."[38]

In another small act to strengthen the independence of the presidency, Cleveland stopped the practice of presidents traveling to Capitol Hill to sign bills and instead required Congress to send newly passed laws to him in the White House so he could study them more carefully before making a decision. This small change may seem trivial on the surface, but it said much about Cleveland's view of the office of the presidency, that it should not be subordinated to Congress and should act with a greater degree of independence than that which had been exhibited in recent decades. It also further validates Cleveland as a strong president and not the timid and weak chief executive he is too often portrayed in the history books.

In the end, it is important to note that Cleveland used the *legal* powers of the presidency to control the egos on Capitol Hill. These fights certainly restored the presidency to its distinguished position in the federal government but, more importantly, he did not strengthen the office by encroaching on the constitutional duties of Congress, like Lincoln did and many other presidents would after him. In short, he did not allow the office to become an "imperial presidency."

SECOND TERM POLITICAL CATASTROPHE

With the onset of the Panic of 1893, the nation's economy was a disaster, followed quickly by the fate of the Democratic Party. The contrasts between Cleveland's first term, where he enjoyed complete party unity, and his second, when the party was on the verge of collapse, could not be starker. It all began over silver and whether or not the country wanted the free coinage of silver or to remain on the gold standard. To help alleviate the country's economic ills, the Democratic Congress, which had repealed the Sherman Silver Purchase Act in August 1893, passed a modest silver bill, the Bland Act in March 1894, that would have coined the silver bullion already in the treasury and put it into circulation. Silverite members were not asking for more silver purchases, only to use that which already existed and was sitting in government vaults. They thought it a reasonable initiative. But to Cleveland and the "gold bugs" it was still more inflation and consistent with the concept of economic planning, in this case fighting inflationary depressions with more inflation.

To make matters worse, this bill seemed to be more for political purposes than economic ones. A congressional delegation from the South and West, the areas earnestly seeking inflationary silver, paid a visit to Cleveland at the White House to urge him to sign the bill, mainly for the purpose of party unity. They believed that the party would take a beating at the polls during the fall midterm campaign if he did not sign the bill and therefore show silver Democrats that he was on their side, at least to some degree. The president exploded at their suggestion and gave them such a tongue-lashing that Senator William Stewart of Nevada wrote a friend of the meeting, "I never had a man talk like that to me in my life." When Cleveland vetoed the bill, many Democrats came unglued and the party nearly imploded, but he acted based on what he believed was best for the country and the economy, not on crass political expediency.[39]

As he entered the final year of his presidency, Grover Cleveland must have been the loneliest man in the world. Scarcely has a nation's chief executive felt as alone as he did, both politically and physically. The economic depression and the policies he enacted to fix it were extremely unpopular in his own party and across the country. Members of Congress refused to visit him, even his fellow Democrats, but he cared not at all. It was "very seldom that a Democratic Senator was seen at the White House," wrote Senator Shelby M. Cullom, an Illinois Republican who admired Cleveland. "The president became completely estranged from the members of his party in both House and Senate, but it seemed to bother him little. He went ahead doing his duty as he saw it, utterly disregarding the wishes of the members of his party in Congress."[40]

Postmaster General William L. Wilson wrote in his diary on February 1, 1896: "It must seem strange to other governments that we have in this country an administration practically without a party to support it." The president "has few to defend or comfort him." Even Cleveland recognized his own deep unpopularity with Congress. "Think of it! Not a man in the Senate with whom I can be on terms of absolute confidence," he wrote to Ambassador Thomas F. Bayard in London. "Not one of them comes to me on public business unless sent for, and then full of reservations and doubts." But Wilson admired his boss and friend. "What a strong, steady, conscientious worker the president is, doing each day's duty courageously and earnestly, and yet maligned and slandered perhaps as no president, perhaps as no public man ever was in all our history."[41]

In addition to his strict monetary policy, his non-jingoistic foreign policy also annoyed people and politicians on both sides of the aisle. Henry Adams, who, unlike his friends and family, supported Cleveland for president, was especially angry and wanted action in Cuba. Adams saw oppression around the globe, in Cuba and in Turkey, where an uprising among Armenians had recently been crushed. "Could not the very gentlemanly and refined philanthropist who rules us in the White House," Adams sarcastically wrote to a friend, "and who, as far as I know, has no function in office except to give our moral support to every infernal corruption on the devil's footstool of which he and his Spanish and Turkish friends are making the earth...." But for Cleveland, the presidency was not about philanthropy or supporting uprisings around the world; it was about protecting Americans at home.[42]

In the end, Cleveland's tough stand on principle cost the party dearly at the ballot box. In the midterm elections in 1894, the Democrats, who had finally gained control of both houses in 1892 for the first time since James Buchanan, were trounced. Republicans kept control of the House until 1910, the Senate until 1912, and held the White House for the next sixteen years. Jeffersonian government was finished in America.

THE FUTURE OF CLEVELAND'S PARTY

After turning down requests to seek a third term in 1896, Cleveland retired from public life. Progressive Democrat William Jennings Bryan gained the presidential nomination and lost to William McKinley, but, more importantly, began the change that transformed the Party of Jefferson to one of centralized governmental power.

From the moment Chief Justice Melville Fuller administered the oath of office to William McKinley, the incoming Republican chief executive, began the end of an era, the era of limited government, the era of our founding principles, the end of Jeffersonian America. From that moment on, the United States, with very few exceptions, would live under progressive government. The question would no longer be how to keep the government smaller but how to grow it larger. Washington would be, forever more, administered on the basis of a more energetic, more powerful centralized system, where the federal government reigned supreme over the states and the people.

With Bryan's ascension to the top leadership role, the Democratic Party began its move to the left, severely bitten by the progressive bug. In three of the next four presidential contests, the party nominated Bryan to head the ticket. Cleveland and Bryan did not see eye-to-eye politically, as each controlled separate wings of the party, a disagreement that eventually split the National Democracy wide open and kept them from power for sixteen years. Cleveland was the leader of the Bourbons – conservatives, or Jeffersonians – who believed in classical liberalism, laissez faire capitalism, economy and accountability in government, sound money, individual responsibility, and a strict construction of the Constitution.

Though originally a Populist, Bryan headed what would become the Progressive wing, those who advocated more taxation, more spending, inflationary currency, and more government intervention in the lives of the people. The rupture was so decisive that Cleveland and Bryan remained at war with each other from 1895 until Cleveland's death in 1908. And with Bryan's ascension to party leadership in 1896, the Democratic Party has never returned to its philosophical roots, the principles of Mr. Jefferson. At least one Cleveland cabinet member saw Bryan's movement as socialism, and even Cleveland himself was deeply suspicious of him, noting that he "has not even the remotest notion of the principles of Democracy."[43]

Spending his retirement years back in his native state of New Jersey, Cleveland was aloof from party business but remained concerned for the future of his beloved "Democracy." He wrote letters to friends for the remainder of his life, seeking a defeat of "Bryanism," ideals he considered a "disastrous heresy," and a return to true principles. If those Jeffersonian principles died out, then the Republic could very well die out with it. In 1899, he wrote his friend and former cabinet member Richard Olney. "And the poor old Democratic party! What a spectacle it presents as a tender to Bryanism and nonsense!" The party had a chance to right itself and win back the presidency in 1900, he believed, if Bryan and his followers were purged. "The Democratic party, if it was only in tolerable condition, could win an easy victory next year; but I am afraid it will never be in winning condition until we have had a regular knock-down fight among ourselves, and succeeded in putting the organization in Democratic hands and reviving Democratic principles in our platform." If not, the nation would get the same candidates that were on the ballot four years before, both very similar in many respects. "Bryanism and McKinleyism!" he wrote with a sarcastic tone. "What a choice for a patriotic American!"[44]

Old-line Democrats around the country wrote him to ask for his support and aid in restoring Jeffersonian conservatism to the party. He always declined to actively participate, for Bryan controlled the party, or "new Democracy," as he termed it. Cleveland knew he was not welcome at any party functions because "I have not been forgiven by Mr. Bryan for lack of support in 1896." And he had no intention of supporting Bryan in 1900 either. Why should he speak out on a "return to the old faith" and to "reorganize under the old banners" when all it would do is increase "the volume of abuse which for a long time has been hurled at my 'defenseless head.'"[45]

But Jeffersonian Democrats wanted him to run for president in 1900 and 1904 to rid the party of Bryanism. The calls were so strong that he had to publicly repudiate them. Many realized that he had been right in his strict conservative policies and that the party and the country were both on the wrong track. The push was, in fact, so strong in 1904 that it concerned President Theodore Roosevelt, who was seeking a term in his own right after assuming the presidency in September 1901 upon McKinley's tragic assassination. "It is evident he has the presidential bee in his bonnet," TR wrote Henry Cabot Lodge about the possibility of a Cleveland candidacy, "and it is equally evident that a large number of people are desirous of running him again. Bryan would bolt him, but in spite of this I think he would be a very formidable candidate." There seemed to be "a great wave of Cleveland sentiment." In two other letters to Lodge, Roosevelt expressed his opinion that a Cleveland candidacy would be "formidable."[46]

Such a campaign would be formidable because Cleveland would seek to give the nation a clear choice between Rooseveltian Progressivism and Jeffersonian Conservatism, and would not follow the "me-tooism" of Bryan, which is where he saw the situation with the Democratic Party in 1900. "My feeling is that the safety of the country is in the rehabilitation of the old Democratic party," he wrote a supporter. "It would be a difficult task to do this," if Bryan prevailed, leading to "absurdities for which the Democratic party would be held responsible." The "old guard" had to "defeat Bryanism and the sham Democratic organization gathered about him." It had to be done or both the party and country might be doomed.[47]

CLEVELAND VS. ROOSEVELT

No two philosophies of government were more diametrically opposed since the days of Jefferson and Hamilton than those of Grover Cleveland and Theodore Roosevelt. As the 20th century approached, and the new progressive philosophy of government gained ground, there came a change in the role of the president in public life. Whereas Cleveland wanted to keep the presidency limited in scope, chief executives after Cleveland, like Teddy Roosevelt, began to take a more active part in the administration of national affairs.

Cleveland idolized Jefferson and believed, as did most early Americans, that the president should not take an overly active role in the government but remain within the strict limits placed on the office by the Constitution. On the other hand, Roosevelt Progressives revered Hamilton and Lincoln, as well as many European tyrants, such as Oliver Cromwell. Once in office, they fundamentally altered the limited nature of the presidency, transforming it from a constitutional image suited to Jefferson to a more powerful one envisioned by Hamilton and personified by Lincoln, where it has remained ever since, save the Harding and Coolidge years. Roosevelt and his successors thus gave shape to the modern presidency.

The Rooseveltian transformation of the presidency also struck another blow at federalism with a more vigorous Lincolnian exercise of power over the states. In his autobiography, Roosevelt wrote that "in all national matters, of importance to the whole people, the nation is to be supreme over state, county, and town alike." Such notions would have horrified Jefferson, just as they did Cleveland.[48]

Cleveland held a strict constructionist view of the Constitution and a narrow Jeffersonian interpretation of the constitutional powers of the presidency. He rightly recognized that the Constitution restricted power; it did not expand it. Roosevelt turned that notion on its head, believing that the president "was limited only by specific restrictions and prohibitions appearing in the Constitution or imposed by the Congress under its Constitutional powers." Roosevelt "declined to adopt the view that what was imperatively necessary for the nation could not be done by the president unless he could find some specific authorization to do it," which was the conservative view held by Jefferson and Cleveland. "My belief," Roosevelt wrote:

> was that it was not only his right but his duty to do anything that the needs of the nation demanded unless such action was forbidden by the Constitution or by the laws. Under this interpretation of executive power I did and caused to be done many things not previously done by the president and the heads of the departments. I did not usurp power, but I did greatly broaden the use of executive power. In other words, I acted for the public welfare, I acted for the common well-being of all our people, whenever and in whatever manner was necessary, unless prevented by direct constitutional or legislative prohibition.[49]

In truth, Roosevelt did usurp power and his progressive view of national and presidential power has prevailed in our time, while Cleveland's Jeffersonian view has died away. And as a result of Roosevelt's power grab, the United States slowly but surely began a march toward a strong centralized state with all power held in Washington.

Mark Twain, a steadfast and loyal Cleveland supporter, understood just how much the party, and the country, needed the former president, especially after Roosevelt's rise to power. When Cleveland was asked to consider another presidential run, and as the Democratic Party began what looked to be another losing presidential campaign with Bryan, Twain wrote to his daughter of his affection for the former president. Cleveland was "a most noble public servant—and in that capacity he has been utterly without blemish," the great author wrote. "Of all our public men of today he stands first in my reverence & admiration, and the next one stands two hundred twenty-fifth. He is the only statesman we have, now. Cleveland *drunk* is a more valuable asset to this country than the whole batch of the rest of our public men *sober*. He is high-minded; all his impulses are great and pure and fine. I wish we had another of this sort."[50]

But no other sort emerged, and at his advanced age Cleveland was simply not up to the task. There would be no great electoral battle between Cleveland and Roosevelt, for he turned down offers in 1900 and 1904. In 1908 talk emerged yet again of a Cleveland candidacy, but the former president died in June of that year. Bryan captured the presidential nomination in 1908 for the third time, but again lost the race, this time to Roosevelt's handpicked successor William Howard Taft. The future of Cleveland's party was set, as progressivism would carry the Democrats into the future. The ideological disaster was so apparent to many old Cleveland conservatives that in 1909 one wrote that the "Democratic party, as we knew it, is dead."[51]

Endnotes

1   Elihu Root, "Introduction," in Robert McElroy, *Grover Cleveland: The Man and the Statesman*, 2 volumes (New York: Harper & Brothers, 1923), I, x, xi.

2   Edgar K. Apgar to Cleveland, August 23, 1882, in Parker, *Recollections*, 49–50.

3   Cleveland to William E. W. Ross and Robert G. King, December 18, 1885, Nevins, *Letters*, 97; Cleveland to George W. Curtis, October 24, 1884, *Ibid.*, 47; Cleveland to Herbert P. Bass, September 30, 1885, *Ibid.*, 80-1; Cleveland to Wilson S. Bissell, December 24, 1885, *Ibid.*, 98; *Buffalo Daily Courier*, August 10, 1884.

4   Cleveland, Letter Accepting Nomination for President, August 18, 1884, Parker, *Writings and Speeches*, 9–13.

5   Cleveland to Wilson S. Bissell, November 13, 1884, Nevins, *Letters*, 48; Brodsky, 108.

6   Cleveland to D-Cady Herrick, July 26, 1891, Cleveland to Michael D. Harter, August 3, 1891, and Cleveland to Governor William E. Russell, July 23, 1891, Nevins, *Letters*, 263–5.

7   Robert Lincoln O'Brien, "Cleveland as Seen by His Stenographer, July, 1892–November, 1895," *Proceedings of the Massachusetts Historical Society* (Oct 1950–May 1953), 142; Cullom, 225–6; Andrew Dickson White, *The Autobiography of Andrew Dickson White*, 2 volumes. (New York: The Century Co., 1904), I, 207.

8   Wilson Diary, May 12, 1896, 82.

9   Cleveland, First Annual Message to Congress (Second Term), December 4, 1893, Richardson, ed., *Messages and Papers*, XII, 5866-5892; List of Presidential Vetoes, http://www.presidency.ucsb.edu/data/vetoes.php.

10   Cleveland, Veto of an Appropriation for Celebrating Decoration Day, May 8, 1882, in Parker, *Writings and Speeches*, 433-435; Armitage, 117; *Buffalo Daily Courier*, May 9, 1882.

11   Jeffers, 48-9; Armitage, 120-1.

12   Armitage, 121-2.

13   *Ibid.*, 125-6; Jeffers, 48-9.

14   Cleveland, Veto Messages, *Public Papers*, I, 28-9, 35-6, 103-27.

15 Jeffers, 67-68; McElroy, I, 51; Cleveland, Veto Messages, *Public Papers*, I, 64-6, 38-9, 68-9; *Albany Evening Journal*, April 10, 1883.

16 Cleveland, Veto Message, Assembly Bill No. 360, For Relief of Surviving Members of First Regiment, N.Y. Mexican Volunteers, *Public Papers*, I, April 25, 1883, 79-80.

17 Carter, *Historical Statistics*, V, 80-81; Cleveland, Second Annual Message (First Term), Richardson, ed., *Messages and Papers*, XI, 5082-5114.

18 Cleveland, Veto of the River and Harbor Bill, May 29, 1896, Richardson, ed., *Messages and Papers*, XIII, 6109-11.

19 Jeffers, 186.

20 Thomas Jefferson to W. H. Torrance, June 11, 1815, in *Writings of Thomas Jefferson*, XIV, 302-6; Jefferson to Abigail Adams, September 11, 1804, in Lester J. Cappon, ed., *The Adams-Jefferson Letters: The Complete Correspondence between Thomas Jefferson & Abigail & John Adams* (Chapel Hill: University of North Carolina Press, 1987), 278-280.

21 James Madison, Veto Message, March 3, 1817, Richardson, ed., *Messages and Papers*, II, 569-70.

22 Franklin Pierce, First Inaugural Address, March 4, 1853, Richardson, ed., *Messages and Papers*, VI, 2730-6; Pierce, Veto Message, May 3, 1854, *Ibid.*, 2782.

23 Cleveland, First Inaugural Address, March 4, 1885, Richardson, ed., *Messages and Papers*, X, 4884-4888.

24 McElroy, I, 52; *New York Times*, March 3, 1883.

25 Burrows and Wallace, 1056; Cleveland, Veto Message, Assembly Bill No. 58, To Regulate Fares on Elevated Railroads in New York City, *Public Papers*, I, 47.

26 White, I, 207; Parker, *Recollections*, 62.

27 Brodsky, 59; *Albany Evening Journal*, March 2, 1883; *New York Times*, March 3, 1883.

28 *New York Herald*, March 3, 1883.

29 Hoar, II, 46.

30 Henry Adams, "The Session," *North American Review*, Vol. 111, No. 228 (July 1870), 29-62.

31 Hoar, II, 46.

32 Welch, 53.

33 Grover Cleveland, "The Independence of the Executive," *Presidential Problems*, 43; Louis Fisher, "Grover Cleveland Against the Senate," *Congressional Studies: A Journal of the Congress*, United States Capitol Historical Society (1979), 13; John F. Marszalek, Jr., "Grover Cleveland and the Tenure of Office Act," *Duquesne Review* (Spring 1970), 209. The removals were: 278 postmasters, 151 commercial officials, 71 in financial posts, 62 in the judiciary, and 81 in the Interior Department. See Fisher, 13.

34 Welch, 54-55; Selig Adler, "Senator Edmund's Part in the Tenure of Office Battle," *Mississippi Valley Historical Review* (December 1945), 393; Fisher, 11.

35 Cleveland to Silas W. Burt, January 28, 1886, Richard Watson Gilder, ed., "Cleveland and the Civil-Service Reformers: His Attitude as Shown in Letters to a Friend." *Century Magazine*, August 1912, LXXXIV, No. 4, 626-627.

36 Cleveland, Special Message to the Senate, March 1, 1886, Richardson ed., *Messages and Papers*, X, 4960-4968; Cleveland to Burt, January 28, 1886, "Civil Service Letters" in *Century Magazine*, 627; Marszalek, 216.

37 Hoar, II, 142-143; Leigh, 53.

38 Dean Acheson, *A Democrat Looks At His Party* (New York: Harper & Brothers, 1955), 39; Welch, 53, 56; Adler, 397. In 1926, the United States Supreme Court, headed by former President William Howard Taft, adopted Cleveland's position. In *Myers v. United States*, by a 6 to 3 vote, the Court ruled the original Tenure of Office Act an unconstitutional violation of the separation powers. See Kermit L. Hall, ed., *The Oxford Companion to the Supreme Court of the United States* (New York, 1992), 569-570.

39 J. Rogers Hollingsworth, *The Whirligig of Politics: The Democracy of Cleveland and Bryan* (Chicago: University of Chicago Press, 1963), 26

40 Cullom, 269.

41 Wilson Diary, February 1, 1896, 19–20; Cleveland to Ambassador Thomas F. Bayard, February 13, 1895, Nevins, *Letters*, 377; Wilson Diary, March 4, 1896, 39.

42 Henry Adams to William Woodville Rockhill, September 10, 1896, in Harold Dean Carter, ed., *Henry Adams and his Friends: A Collection of His Unpublished Letters* (Boston: Houghton Mifflin Company, 1947), 386.

43 Wilson Diary, May 30, 1896, 93; Parker, *Recollections*, 209

44   Cleveland to Wilson S. Bissell, September 16, 1900, Nevins, *Letters*, 536–7; Cleveland to Richard Olney, March 19, 1899 and April 12, 1899, *Ibid.*, 512–3; Cleveland to Charles S. Hamlin, September 13, 1900, *Ibid.*, 536.

45   Cleveland to Judson B. Harmon, July 17, 1900, *Ibid.*, 532–3; Cleveland to Wilson S. Bissell, September 16, 1900, *Ibid.*, 536–7.

46   Theodore Roosevelt to Henry Cabot Lodge, May 4, 1903, May 11, 1903, and May 23, 1903, Henry Cabot Lodge, *Selections from the Correspondence of Theodore Roosevelt and Henry Cabot Lodge, 1884–1918.* 2 volumes. (New York: Charles Scribner's Sons, 1925), II, 13, 17.

47   Cleveland to Judson B. Harmon, July 17, 1900, Nevins, *Letters*, 532–3.

48   Roosevelt, *Autobiography*, 607–8.

49   *Ibid.*, 614.

50   Mark Twain to Jean Clemens, June 19, 1908, Mark Twain Papers, University of California, Berkeley.

51   Merrill, 207.

Afterword

WHY HISTORY MATTERS

"History, by apprising them of the past, will enable them to judge the future; it will avail them of the experience of other times and other nations; it will qualify them as judges of the actions and designs of men; it will enable them to know ambition under every disguise it may assume; and knowing it, to defeat its views."

—Thomas Jefferson, *Notes on the State of Virginia*

"It is well in these latter days to often turn back and read of the faith which the founders of our party had in the people—how exactly they approached their needs and with what lofty aims and purposes they sought the public good."

—Cleveland to Herbert Bissell, September 30, 1885

In 1816, in a letter to John Adams, Thomas Jefferson wrote an interesting, even puzzling sentence for modern Americans. "I like the dreams of the future better than the history of the past," he said to his old revolutionary friend. This would seem to suggest that the Sage of Monticello disliked history and saw no positive benefit to be gained from its study. Indeed, as Jefferson wrote in 1807 while serving as president, "History, in general, only informs us what bad government is." But one must see the world through Jefferson's eyes. As he looked into the past he saw nothing but darkness and tyranny. To him the future held so much more promise than a dreadful, tyrannical past.[1]

But Jefferson did understand that future Americans would derive tremendous benefits from studying those who came before them. As he wrote in his only book, *Notes on the State of Virginia*, "History, by apprising them of the past, will enable them to judge the future; it will avail them of the experience of other times and other nations; it will qualify them as judges of the actions and designs of men; it will enable them to know ambition under every disguise it may assume; and knowing it, to defeat its views." For him it was always about keeping the government in check and that could only come by studying the past. "History has informed us that bodies of men, as well as individuals, are susceptible of the spirit of tyranny," he wrote in "A Summary View of the Rights of British America." It is advice we should pay heed.[2]

At first glance, though, it might seem odd to many that a nineteenth-century president, like Grover Cleveland, could have any bearing on the modern world. How could the record of a president who served more than a century ago have any influence on contemporary politics or impact Americans today? Why should we even care about earlier presidents and what happened in bygone eras?

Many economists, politicians, and pundits believe there's nothing to gain from studying the past. We live in a new world, they often say, and should look to the future and to new ideas. But that is where we make a great mistake. We need only to look to the past to what worked and to those principles that made the United States the greatest nation on Earth. There are lessons we as a society can learn by viewing modern times through the prism of history, and particularly for those who consider themselves conservatives can gain much by examining the public career of Grover Cleveland, one of the most principled public men in American history.

"For conservatism is grounded in the past," writes Pat Buchanan. "Its principles are derived from the Constitution, experience, history, tradition, custom, and the wisdom of those who have gone before us – 'The best that has been thought and said.' It does not purport to know the future. It is about preserving the true, the good, the beautiful."[3]

As Chuck Norris wrote in his book, *Black Belt Patriotism*, "Go back to go forward." But perhaps our Lord said it best in Jeremiah 6:16: "Stand at the crossroads and look; ask for the ancient paths, ask where the good way is, and walk in it, and you will find rest for your souls."[4]

But rarely do we hear political candidates discuss our glorious past. Today's leaders express new ideas, new solutions, and new ways of doing things, trying to impress voters with how innovative they are when we should be looking for our answers in the past, at the old ways of doing things. For this reason, we study history. To students, both past and present, as well as those in the future, history should not be seen as simply a bunch of facts, names, and dates; nor is it, as one critic suggested, "Just one damn thing after another." The study of history has a purpose. We must learn from it because if we don't, we become irrelevant as a people and as a great civilization.[5]

Ronald Reagan reminded the American people in his 1989 Farewell Address, "If we forget what we did, we won't know who we are." How right he was. Consider for a moment an absence of history. What if we had no knowledge of the past, no stories, no facts, no records, nothing but ignorance? What if we knew nothing that had happened before our lifetimes and beyond the grasp of our memories or that of our elders? A scary thought indeed.[6]

History can intellectually enrich one's life and can be an excellent guide to understanding present events and to correct existing problems. "What is the solution to our current woes?" asks Professor Larry Schweikart in his book *What Would the Founders Say? A Patriot's Answers to America's Most Pressing Problems*. "It helps, when you are lost, to find out where you made the wrong turn. But if you don't know where you started, how can you discover where you went off course?" The study of our history will show us the answers, allowing us to understand where we have come from as a society so we will know where we are going as a society. So, it is important that the study of history, as well as the writing of it, reflects modern times.[7]

A thorough understanding of American history can also make one a better citizen and a more enlightened voter. Grover Cleveland would have agreed. He held strongly to what he believed, passionately advocating the principles of Jeffersonian conservatism, ideals that came out of the American Revolution and was, in his day, advocated by the Democratic Party. He believed those standards should be freely championed, not concealed or watered down, while the history of those beliefs could be an excellent judge for the present and future. "The Democratic cause need have no fear of the most complete discussion of its principles, and the history of its great leaders and their achievements cannot fail to inspire the members of the party with pride and veneration," he wrote a friend during his first year as president. "It is well in these latter days to often turn back and read of the faith which the founders of our party had in the people – how exactly they approached their needs and with what lofty aims and purposes they sought the public good."[8]

It is Grover Cleveland's presidency that we can learn from and emulate. He is the quintessential president for Jeffersonians to admire. When Grover Cleveland's great public career ended on March 4, 1897, one of his cabinet officers, Postmaster General William L. Wilson, confided to his diary, asking, "When will another Cleveland occupy the White House?"[9]

We have been waiting for more than one hundred years, but let us pray for our sakes and that of posterity that the wait will soon be over.

Endnotes

1   Thomas Jefferson to John Adams, August 1, 1816, Cappon, ed., *Adams-Jefferson Letters*, 483-485; Thomas Jefferson to John Norvell, June 14, 1807, in Ford, ed., *Works*, X, 416.

2   Jefferson, *Notes on the State of Virginia*, in Peterson, comp., *Jefferson: Writings*, 274.

3   Patrick J. Buchanan, *Day of Reckoning: How Hubris, Ideology, and Greed Are Tearing America Apart* (New York: Thomas Dunne Books, 2007), 86.

4   Chuck Norris, *Black Belt Patriotism: How to Reawaken America* (Washington: Fidelis, 2008).

5   This quote is most often attributed to Henry Ford.

6   Ronald Reagan, Farewell Address, January 11, 1989, http://www.reagan.utexas.edu/archives/speeches/1989/011189i.htm.

7   Larry Schweikart, *What Would the Founders Say? A Patriot's Answers to America's Most Pressing Problems* (New York: Sentinel Books, 2011), 9.

8   Grover Cleveland to Herbert Bissell, September 30, 1885, Nevins, *Letters*, 80-1.

9   Wilson Diary, March 4, 1897, 250.

About The Author

RYAN S. WALTERS is a writer and an independent historian. He is currently the book review editor at the Abbeville Institute and teaches American history at Collin College in North Texas where he lives with his wife Candice and mini dachshund Molly. He is the author of Remember Mississippi and Apollo 1.

Index

A.

Acheson, Dean 137, 147

Allison, William B. 78, 93

Altgeld, John 85

Anson, Cap 27

Apgar, Edgar K. 122, 145

Arthur, Chester A. 28, 32, 89, 93, 101

B.

Bailey, Thomas 115, 119

Barry, David S. 27, 40, 89, 97

Barton, Clara 47

Bassett, Richard 7

Bayard, Thomas F. 7, 8, 16, 105, 139, 148

Beatty, Jack 16, 47, 70

Bissell, Wilson S. 16, 32, 123, 145, 148, 149, 153

Blaine, James G. 21, 23, 28, 40, 106, 107

Blount, James H. 107

Borden 71

Brodsky, Alyn 16, 40, 66, 67, 73, 123, 145, 147

Bryan, William Jennings 62, 78, 86, 88, 89, 96, 112, 140, 141, 142, 144, 148

Buchanan, James 1, 88, 139

Buchanan, Patrick J. 112, 139, 150

Burnett, John D. 135

Burrows, Edwin 29, 40, 40, 132, 146

Bush 41

Butler, Ben 25

C.

Calhoun, John C. 19

Cannon, Joe 62

Carlisle, John 62, 73, 89

Catchings, Thomas 67, 90, 97

Clark, Champ 3

Coxey, Jacob 45

Cromwell, Oliver 142

Cullom, Shelby 6, 7, 16, 61, 73, 82, 96, 97, 124, 138, 145, 148

D.

Daniels, Josephus 3, 15, 88, 89, 97, 97

Darwin, Charles 102

Davis, Jefferson 2, 5, 10

DiLorenzo, Thomas 54, 71, 72

Duskin, George M. 135

F.

Foraker, Joseph B. 9

Fuller, Melville 10, 91, 140

G.

Garfield, James A. 21, 24, 28, 39, 44, 105, 137

Garland, Augustus 4, 5, 15, 135, 136

Gilder, Richard Watson 118, 147

Gompers, Samuel 52

Goode, John 68, 73

Goodyear, Charles 22, 39

Gordon, John B. 10

Gordon 87

Gould, Jay 39, 72, 73, 81, 88, 132, 133

H.

Halpin, Maria 22, 23

Harrison, Benjamin 24, 26, 58, 59, 60, 61, 65, 72, 80, 91, 92, 93, 95, 106, 107, 108, 109

Harter, Michael D. 82, 145

Hawley, Joseph 9

Hayes, Rutherford B. 4, 29, 40, 45, 70, 72, 137

Herbert, Hilary 8, 114

Higgs, Robert 96, 97

Hoar, George F. 5, 6, 7, 134

Hofstadter, Richard 25, 39

Hoover, Ike 26, 28, 29

J.

Johnson, Andrew 7, 77, 105, 134, 135, 136

Johnston, Albert Sidney 11

K.

Kelly, John 25

Kipling, Rudyard 102

L.

LaFollette, Robert M. 62

Lamar, L. Q. C. 5, 6, 7

Lamont, Daniel 25, 26

Leigh, Philip 137

Lincoln, Abraham 1, 2, 5, 7, 10, 23, 24, 26, 28, 39, 40, 47, 56, 62, 72, 76, 86, 89, 124, 133, 137, 142, 145

M.

Mahan, Alfred Thayer 103, 104

McClanahan, Brion 8

McCune, Charles 22

McKinley, William 59, 60, 62, 72, 85, 86, 93, 108, 110, 111, 112, 140, 141

Morgan, H. Wayne 57

Morgan, J. P. 84, 85, 132

Morgan, John 90

Morris, Roy 29

Morrison, William R. 56

N.

Nevins, Allan 26, 32, 71, 72, 73, 85, 108

Norris, Chuck 150

O.

Olney 109, 114, 115, 141

P.

Parker, George F. 35, 54

Pendel, Thomas 26

Polk, James K. 10, 26

R.

Reagan, Ronald 151

Reed, Thomas "Czar" 59, 60

Rhodes, Cecil 102

Rockefeller, John D. 88

Roosevelt, Franklin D. 93, 94

Roosevelt, Theodore 10, 24, 26, 27, 52, 61, 93, 101, 103, 104, 111, 112, 121, 132, 141, 142, 143, 144

Root, Elihu 121

Rothbard, Murray 79, 84

Russell, William E. 38

S.

Salisbury, Lord 114, 115

Schurz, Carl 21, 80, 86

Schweikart, Larry 151

Scorsese, Martin 29

Seymour, Horatio 20, 78

Shearman, Thomas 87, 88

Sherman, John 61, 92

Sherman, William T. 9

Sinclair, Winston 12

Smith, Hoke 4, 88

Steffens, Lincoln 24

Stevens, John 106, 107

Stevenson, Adlai 37, 37

Stewart, William M. 7, 138

T.

Taft, William Howard 144

Talbot, George 31, 32

Tilden, Samuel J. 4, 20

Trotter, James Monroe 13

Twain, Mark 143, 144

Tweed, "Boss" 29, 29, 29, 29, 29, 29, 32

Tyler, John 105

V.

Van Buren 93, 94

Vanderbilt, William H. 132

Vilas, William 37, 62, 108

Villard, Henry 80

W.

Wallace, Mike 29, 132

Watterson, Henry 3, 4

Welch, Richard 57, 79, 137

Westerfield, Ray 77

Weyler, Valeriano 110

Whitney, William 101

Wilson, William 8, 86, 88, 139, 152

Wilson, Woodrow 3, 4, 39, 70, 89, 90, 101

Woods 5

Woodville 148

Woodward 11, 12, 17

www.ingramcontent.com/pod-product-compliance
Lightning Source LLC
Chambersburg PA
CBHW060048100426
42742CB00014B/2742